10

W9-BXY-885

10
Understanding American History

The Civil Rights Movement

Lydia Bjornlund

Bruno Leone
Series Consultant

ReferencePoint Press®

San Diego, CA

© 2013 ReferencePoint Press, Inc.
Printed in the United States

For more information, contact:
ReferencePoint Press, Inc.
PO Box 27779
San Diego, CA 92198
www.ReferencePointPress.com

LIBRARY OF CONGRESS CATALOGING-IN-PUBLICATION DATA

Bjornlund, Lydia D.
  The civil rights movement / by Lydia Bjornlund.
      p. cm. -- (The understanding American history series)
  Includes bibliographical references and index.
  ISBN-13: 978-1-60152-478-2 (hardback)
  ISBN-10: 1-60152-478-1 (hardback)
  1. Civil rights movements--United States--Juvenile literature. 2. African Americans--Civil rights--Juvenile literature. 3. United States--Race relations--Juvenile literature. [1. African Americans--Civil rights--Juvenile literature.] I. Title.
  E185.61.B56 2012
  323.1196'073--dc23
                                                                                      2012011560

Contents

Foreword

America's Puritan ancestors—convinced that their adopted country was blessed by God and would eventually rise to worldwide prominence—proclaimed their new homeland the shining "city upon a hill." The nation that developed since those first hopeful words were uttered has clearly achieved prominence on the world stage and it has had many shining moments but its history is not without flaws. The history of the United States is a virtual patchwork of achievements and blemishes. For example, America was originally founded as a New World haven from the tyranny and persecution prevalent in many parts of the Old World. Yet the colonial and federal governments in America took little or no action against the use of slave labor by the southern states until the 1860s, when a civil war was fought to eliminate slavery and preserve the federal union.

In the decades before and after the Civil War, the United States underwent a period of massive territorial expansion; through a combination of purchase, annexation, and war, its east–west borders stretched from the Atlantic to the Pacific Oceans. During this time, the Industrial Revolution that began in eighteenth-century Europe found its way to America, where it was responsible for considerable growth of the national economy. The United States was now proudly able to take its place in the Western Hemisphere's community of nations as a worthy economic and technological partner. Yet America also chose to join the major western European powers in a race to acquire colonial empires in Africa, Asia, and the islands of the Caribbean and South Pacific. In this scramble for empire, foreign territories were often peacefully annexed but military force was readily used when needed, as in the Philippines during the Spanish-American War of 1898.

Toward the end of the nineteenth century and concurrent with America's ambitions to acquire colonies, its vast frontier and expanding industrial base provided both land and jobs for a new and ever-growing wave of immigrants from southern and eastern Europe. Although America had always encouraged immigration, these newcomers—Italians, Greeks, and eastern European Jews, among others—were seen as different from the vast majority of earlier immigrants, most of whom were from northern and western Europe. The presence of these newcomers was treated as a matter of growing concern, which in time evolved into intense opposition. Congress boldly and with calculated prejudice set out to create a barrier to curtail the influx of unwanted nationalities and ethnic groups to America's shores. The outcome was the National Origins Act, passed in 1924. That law severely reduced immigration to the United States from southern and eastern Europe. Ironically, while this was happening, the Statue of Liberty stood in New York Harbor as a visible and symbolic beacon lighting the way for people of *all* nationalities and ethnicities seeking sanctuary in America.

Unquestionably, the history of the United States has not always mirrored that radiant beacon touted by the early settlers. As often happens, reality and dreams tend to move in divergent directions. However, the story of America also reveals a people who have frequently extended a helping hand to a weary world and who have displayed a ready willingness—supported by a flexible federal constitution—to take deliberate and effective steps to correct injustices, past and present. America's private and public philanthropy directed toward other countries during times of natural disasters (such as the contributions of financial and human resources to assist Haiti following the January 2010, earthquake) and the legal right to adopt amendments to the US Constitution (including the Thirteenth Amendment freeing the slaves and the Nineteenth Amendment granting women the right to vote) are examples of the nation's generosity and willingness to acknowledge and reverse wrongs.

With objectivity and candor, the titles selected for the Understanding American History series portray the many sides of America, depicting both its shining moments and its darker hours. The series strives to help readers achieve a wider understanding and appreciation of the American experience and to encourage further investigation into America's evolving character and founding principles.

Important Events in the Civil Rights Movement

1896
In *Plessy v. Ferguson* the US Supreme Court rules that providing separate but equal facilities for African Americans is constitutional.

1958
Four black college students begin a sit-in at a segregated Woolworth's lunch counter in Greensboro, North Carolina. The sit-in triggers similar protests at other segregated facilities.

1954
In *Brown v. Board of Education* the US Supreme Court rules that segregation in public schools is unconstitutional.

1900 / **1945** **1950** **1955**

1948
President Harry S. Truman signs an executive order declaring "equality of treatment and opportunity for all persons in the armed services without regard to race, color, religion, or national origin."

1955
Rosa Parks refuses to give up her seat on the bus to a white passenger. Her arrest launches a boycott of buses in Montgomery, Alabama, that will last more than a year.

1957
Nine African American students are blocked by state police from attending Little Rock Central High School, forcing federal troops to step in to offer protection.

1964

President Lyndon B. Johnson signs the Civil Rights Act of 1964, the most sweeping civil rights legislation since Reconstruction. The Civil Rights Act prohibits discrimination of all kinds based on race, color, religion, or national origin and gives the federal government power to enforce desegregation.

1963

About two hundred thousand civil rights demonstrators join the March on Washington, DC, where Martin Luther King Jr. delivers his famous "I Have a Dream" speech.

1968

Martin Luther King Jr. is shot and killed as he stands on the balcony outside his hotel room.

2008

Barack Obama becomes the first African American president of the United States.

1961

More than one thousand student freedom riders take bus trips throughout the South to test new laws that prohibit segregation on interstate travel.

1966

The militant Black Panthers are formed.

| 1960 | 1962 | 1964 | 1966 | 1968 | 2010 |

1962

James Meredith becomes the first black student to enroll at the University of Mississippi. President John F. Kennedy sends federal troops to control the ensuing violence and riots.

1967

Thurgood Marshall becomes the first African American Supreme Court justice.

2006

In *Parents v. Seattle* and *Meredith v. Jefferson* the Supreme Court rules that programs designed to maintain diversity in public schools by considering race are unconstitutional.

1978

In *Regents of the University of California v. Bakke* the Supreme Court upholds the legality of affirmative action by ruling that race can be among the factors considered in choosing a diverse student body, but it outlaws rigid quota systems and point systems.

1965

In an incident dubbed Bloody Sunday, police attack African Americans who are marching from Selma to Montgomery, Alabama, to demand voting rights.

The Defining Characteristics of the Civil Rights Movement

On August 28, 1963, Martin Luther King Jr. stepped up to a podium in front of the Lincoln Memorial and looked out at the huge crowd gathered across the national mall. As a minister who had emerged as the most famous civil rights leader of his day, King was used to speaking to audiences, but this was different. An estimated 250,000 Americans had converged on the nation's capital in what King himself predicted would "go down in history as the greatest demonstration for freedom in the history of our nation."[1]

The crowd gathered on the mall had already heard from some of the most prominent leaders of the civil rights movement. King's speech, the last of the day, is generally considered to be among the best and most powerful speeches in American history. King began by mentioning some of the obstacles that the civil rights movement had overcome, but he soon focused on his dream of the future America:

I have a dream that one day this nation will rise up and live out the true meaning of its creed: "We hold these truths to be self-evident, that all men are created equal." I have a dream that one day on the red hills of Georgia, the sons of former slaves and the sons of former slave owners will be able to sit down together at the table of brotherhood. I have a dream that one day even the state of Mississippi, a state sweltering with the heat of injustice, sweltering with the heat of oppression, will be transformed into an oasis of freedom and justice. I have a dream that my four little children will one day live in a nation where they will not be judged by the color of their skin but by the content of their character. I have a dream today![2]

Thousands gather in Washington, DC, in 1963 to hear the words of Martin Luther King Jr., the civil rights leader who inspired millions over the years with his heartfelt oratory and his dedication to achieving equal rights for African Americans.

King's speech captured the optimism of his listeners. President John F. Kennedy had just introduced legislation calling for equal rights for African Americans, and the demonstrators had come from across the country to show their support. The civil rights movement had come a long way.

The Origins of the Movement

Although it is difficult to name a single event as the beginning of the civil rights movement, many historians cite Rosa Parks's 1954 refusal to give up her seat on a city bus in Montgomery, Alabama, to a white person. Parks's action was courageous; African Americans had been beaten and even killed for refusing to follow the rules of segregation in the Deep South. Her single act of resistance sparked a boycott of city buses throughout the community—a boycott that lasted over a year and ended with the capitulation of the city. Because the majority of bus riders were African American, the boycott hurt the city economically. This type of nonviolent resistance to unfair laws and practices became a defining characteristic of the civil rights movement.

The Montgomery bus boycott proved to be the spark that set the souls of thousands on fire. African Americans—young and old—boycotted buses, stores, and restaurants to demand the right to services that whites took for granted. Although participants in the civil rights movement were primarily African American, some whites joined the cause. At first the demands were modest: they asked to be allowed to eat lunch at the stores where they shopped, to be allowed to remain seated on the bus even if a white person had to stand, to be treated with basic respect. Over time, however, African Americans began to share King's dream of true equality—when a black American would be treated just like any other American, not like a second-class citizen.

A War with Many Fronts

The battle for civil rights was fought on a number of fronts: in the courts, in legislative halls, in the pocketbook, in the streets, and in the media. The National Association for the Advancement of Colored People (NAACP)

Civil Rights Hot Spots

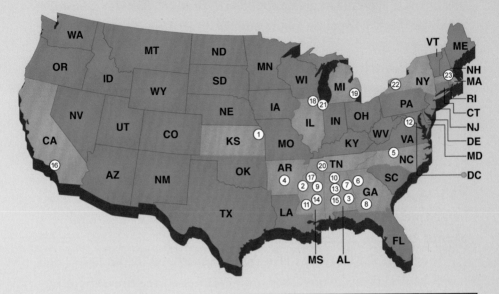

1. Topeka, KS *Brown vs. Board of Education*	13. Birmingham, AL Baptist Church bombing kills 4 African American girls
2. Sumner, MS Emmett Till	14. Philadelphia, MS Activists launch Freedom Summer campaign
3. Montgomery, AL Rosa Parks	15. Selma, AL MLK Jr. marches after Bloody Sunday
4. Little Rock, AR Little Rock Nine	16. Los Angeles, CA Watts riots
5. Greensboro, NC Woolworth's Sit-In	17. Hernando, MS James Meredith shot during "March Against Fear"
6. Atlanta, GA MLK Jr. arrested at sit-in	18. Cicero, IL MLK Jr. and others heckled and assaulted
7. Anniston, AL Freedom Riders assaulted	19. Detroit, MI Rioting leaves 43 dead
8. Albany, GA MLK Jr. arrested with other demonstrators	20. Memphis, TN MLK Jr. assassinated
9. Oxford, MS James Meredith integrates University of Mississippi	21. Chicago, IL Two killed in police raid on Black Panther leader's house
10. Birmingham, AL George Wallace blocks black students at University of Alabama	22. Attica, NY Prison riot
11. Jackson, MS NAACP leader Medgar Evers murdered	23. Boston, MA Rally against school desegregation
12. Washington, DC "I Have a Dream" speech by MLK Jr.	

led the charge in the courts. NAACP lawyers brought suit against public and private organizations to challenge state and local segregation laws. The NAACP achieved its greatest success in *Brown v. Board of Education*, in which the US Supreme Court outlawed racial segregation in public schools.

Civil rights leaders also fought to overturn state and local segregation laws, voting laws, and other laws that prohibited them from exercising their constitutional rights. They also sought to secure new federal legislation that would protect their rights. Legal reform gained ground in the 1960s, culminating with the passage of the Civil Rights Act of 1964 and the Voting Rights Act of 1965. Even after this landmark legislation, however, the civil rights movement continued, fighting the prejudice and discriminatory practices that remained in the very fiber of American communities.

Above all, the battle for civil rights was waged in the hearts and minds of Americans, who—over time—witnessed the brutality of racism and discrimination with an increasingly jaundiced eye. People who once believed in the myth of "separate but equal" schools were riveted to their TVs as they watched black teenagers in Arkansas try to get by armed guards and mobs of whites to enter Little Rock Central High School. Young people became involved directly. Organizations such as the Student Nonviolent Coordinating Committee led programs in which college students spent their summers in the South setting up schools for young people, testing new court rulings and laws that allowed or required desegregated facilities, and registering African Americans to vote.

One of the dominant characteristics of the movement was the emphasis on nonviolence even in the face of armed adversity. Even after African Americans had federal law on their side, states and localities continued to fight to keep segregation intact. Police blockades were set up to stop civil rights marchers from reaching their destination. Governors blocked their entrance to white schools. White supremacist groups firebombed the churches where they came together to plan and to pray. Civil rights leaders—and followers—were killed. Again and again African Americans responded to the violence and intimidation with a sense of calm resolve. When armed police blocked their way over the bridge in Selma, Alabama, the marchers knelt to pray. When they were discouraged, they sang. "We shall overcome" became the anthem of a people who were willing to put their very lives on the line to realize their civil rights.

A New Generation

Over the ensuing decades, new Americans—black and white, young and old—have stepped into the shoes of the first civil rights workers to break down racial barriers. Where the first generation left off, others have continued to make inroads into new positions of leadership in the public and private sectors. In 2008 the United States witnessed the election of the first African American president—a development that only the most optimistic among King's 1963 audience would have dreamed. Today, thanks to the dedication of thousands to fighting injustice, state and local governments have repealed laws supporting, reinforcing, and protecting racism and segregation. Although the legacy of racial segregation has left deep scars, each year the nation and its people heal a bit more from the wounds.

Chapter 1

What Conditions Led to the Civil Rights Movement?

In August 1955 fourteen-year-old Emmett Till, a black youth from Chicago, was visiting his relatives in Mississippi. Emmett and one of his cousins skipped church and joined some other boys to buy candy at Bryant's Grocery. On a dare from his cousins, Emmett spoke to the owner's wife, Carolyn, who was working the cash register. Accounts of what transpired at the store differ. Some said he flirted with Carolyn Bryant; others said he whistled at her. According to Emmett's relatives, he "had a stuttering problem when he had difficulty pronouncing certain words, so his mother taught him to whistle when he couldn't pronounce a word."[3] Carolyn later insisted that he had grabbed her at the waist and asked her for a date. Whatever he said apparently frightened Carolyn Bryant; when she ran out to her car to get a gun, the boys fled.

A couple of nights later, Carolyn's husband Roy and his brother rapped at the door of the relatives' house and demanded to talk to Emmett. Emmett's relatives tried to help the teen escape, but the two men caught him and dragged him from his home. Several days later a fisherman found Emmett's body in the Tallahatchie River, weighed down by a 70-pound fan (32kg). In addition to being shot in the head, his body was badly mutilated. He had been beaten so badly that one side of his skull was crushed. Despite overwhelming evidence of their guilt, Roy Bryant and J.W. Milam were tried for murder and acquitted by an all-white jury. After the trial they bragged publicly about the brutal crime and sold their story to *Life* magazine.

The barbarous murder of Emmett Till was not an isolated incident. Till had broken unwritten rules against associating with a white person. Those rules were supported by a legal system based on racist principles and practices. Throughout the South state and local laws, known as Jim Crow laws, enforced racial segregation in almost all aspects of life and supported a social system in which blacks were subservient. Blacks in northern cities like Chicago, where Emmett Till was from, sometimes suffered less under racism, but blacks rarely had power equal to whites. On the PBS website "The Rise and Fall of Jim Crow," writer Tsahai Tafari explains:

> Racial inequality was not unique to the South. It was the norm across the nation, and other regions of the United States saw similar violence and state-sanctioned discrimination. Though Jim Crow and its specific laws and practices occurred in the South, the system thrived because it was sanctioned by the national government. The actions—or, more frequently, inactions—of the three branches of the federal government were essential in defining the lifespan of Jim Crow."[4]

The Bonds of Slavery

The racism that existed in the United States in the 1950s was born hundreds of years earlier with the institution of slavery. For over two hundred years, until slavery was abolished by the Thirteenth Amendment in 1865, slavery had been a dominant social and economic force in the South. By 1860, the census counted the slave population at 4 million. The slaves had none of the rights accorded to American citizens. Most worked for white owners as domestic servants and farm laborers. The most "enlightened" slave owners typically saw themselves as the caretakers of people who were incapable of taking care of themselves. In the worst circumstances, slaves were considered no better than dogs.

In 1863, during the Civil War, Abraham Lincoln issued the Emancipation Proclamation, which freed all slaves living in states that had seceded from the Union. Two years later, the Thirteenth Amendment extended freedom to all slaves. The Fourteenth Amendment, passed in 1868, guaranteed African Americans equal rights and equal protection; the Fifteenth Amendment, passed in 1870, gave black men the right to vote.

From Slaves to Sharecroppers

The post–Civil War amendments had secured freedom for slaves, but most newly freed blacks had no possessions, no homes, no education, and no means of survival. Following the Civil War the federal government took steps to help African Americans as part of an overall effort to rebuild the South. During the period from 1865 to 1877 known as Reconstruction, the federal government kept troops in the South to protect ex-slaves from violence and to further other political goals.

In 1865 a new federal agency, the Bureau of Refugees, Freedmen, and Abandoned Lands (commonly known as the Freedmen's Bureau) was assigned the responsibility of providing food, clothing, basic health care, and other necessities to the newly freed slaves. The army was put in charge of enforcing Freedmen's Bureau measures. Members of the Freedmen's Bureau helped negotiate terms of employment between the white landowners and the blacks who had once worked as slaves. The bureau also helped set up thousands of schools throughout the South to help ex-slaves learn to read and write. It also established some of the nation's first colleges for blacks, including Howard University. The university took its name from Oliver O. Howard, a Civil War veteran who was tapped to head the Freedmen's Bureau.

Newly freed slaves struggled to build lives amid the deeply entrenched racism of the South. Protected by US troops, African Americans voted and participated in government. Between 1867 and 1877, two African Americans were elected to the Senate and fourteen to the House of Representatives. But attempts to make substantial changes were stymied by the fact that African Americans lacked economic power and the skills to be self-sufficient.

One of the few options available to newly freed slaves was sharecropping, a system of labor in which one group of people—in this case for-

Black slaves pick cotton in the South. Racism in the United States before the start of the civil rights movement was a product of the institution of slavery, which flourished for two hundred years before it was abolished by the Thirteenth Amendment to the Constitution.

mer slaves—is assigned a plot of land to work in exchange for a share of the crops that are grown on that plot. Although the Freedmen's Bureau helped to develop and enforce the sharecropping agreements, share-cropping tended to favor landowners. In addition, because former slaves were uneducated and often illiterate, these contracts often cheated them of their share of the harvest. Throughout the South, this economic arrangement provided no opportunity for African Americans to move off the plantation and resulted in maintaining the status quo. Many of the freedmen were no better off than they had been as slaves.

White Supremacy

Southerners accused the Freedmen's Bureau of inciting blacks to rise up against their former masters. In many former slaveholding counties, African Americans greatly outnumbered whites. To coun-

The Origin of Jim Crow

The term *Jim Crow* is believed to have originated around 1830 when a white minstrel show performer blackened his face with charcoal paste or burnt cork and danced to the Jim Crow tune:

> "Weel about and turn about
> And do just so.
> Every time I weel about
> I jump Jim Crow."

The Jim Crow character was an old, foolish, lame slave—a stereotype that white viewers found amusing. Other minstrel performers began to mimic the original Jim Crow, and by the mid-1850s the act had become one of the most popular minstrel shows not only in the United States but in England and parts of Europe as well. The term *Jim Crow* soon became a racial slur used to describe an ignorant and inferior African American person. By the end of the nineteenth century, the meaning of the term had expanded still further to include the set of laws and customs developed to keep blacks and whites separate and blacks inferior.

Quoted in Diane McWhorter, *A Dream of Freedom: The Civil Rights Movement from 1954 to 1968*. New York: Scholastic, 2004, p. 25.

ter what they viewed as a major threat, whites formed secret societies in which they pledged support for one another and worked to oust politicians who encouraged change. The most famous of these groups was the Ku Klux Klan (KKK), which used terror and violence to enforce the racist order.

From the beginning, one of the first priorities of the Klan was to keep blacks from voting and to keep power out of the hands of Republicans who sought to change the South. Hundreds of blacks were brutally beaten or killed to keep them from voting. Republican organizers and leaders were threatened with violence. Some were assassinated. The Klan also came out during elections, surrounding the polls and intimidating voters.

Reconstruction ended abruptly in 1876, after Republicans agreed to withdraw federal troops from the South in exchange for their candidate, Rutherford B. Hayes, being declared the winner of the contested presidential election. This controversial compromise left southern Democrats in charge of the rebuilding process. Southerners responded by finding ways to revert to a society that was similar to the pre–Civil War period—a society with blacks firmly on the bottom and laws that would keep them there.

Plessy v. Ferguson

In most of the South—throughout the country in fact—life for black Americans in the late 1800s was far different than for whites. In a speech delivered in the Ohio House of Representatives in 1886 and later published as *The Black Laws*, African American legislator Benjamin W. Arnett describes life in segregated Ohio:

> I have traveled in this free country for twenty hours without anything to eat; not because I had no money to pay for it, but because I was colored. Other passengers of a lighter hue had breakfast, dinner and supper. In traveling we are thrown in "jim crow" cars, denied the privilege of buying a berth in the sleeping coach. This monster caste stands at the doors of the theatres and skating rinks, locks the doors of the pews in our fashionable churches, closes the mouths of some of the ministers in their pulpits which prevents the man of color from breaking the bread of life to his fellowmen. This foe of my race stands at the school house door and separates the children, by reason

of "color," and denies to those who have a visible admixture of African blood in them the blessings of a graded [public elementary] school and equal privileges.[5]

One of the first challenges to segregation came in 1892, when Homer Plessy, an African American businessman from Louisiana, bought a first-class ticket to travel in the "whites only" car on a train traveling from New Orleans to Covington, Louisiana. One of Plessy's grandparents was black, but the law classified as black anyone with just one drop of blood from a person with African ancestry. When Plessy refused to move to the car for African Americans, he was arrested and thrown in jail. At a subsequent trial, he was found guilty of violating the state's segregation laws.

Plessy took his case all the way to the US Supreme Court. In 1896 the Supreme Court upheld the right of Louisiana to make and enforce laws about businesses within the state, including laws requiring racial segregation. In the majority opinion, Justice Henry Billings Brown wrote:

The object of the [Fourteenth] amendment was undoubtedly to enforce the absolute equality of the two races before the law, but in the nature of things it could not have been intended to abolish distinctions based upon color, or to enforce social, as distinguished from political equality, or a commingling of the two races upon terms unsatisfactory to either.[6]

The court also upheld the racist concepts that served as the basis for segregation laws. "If one race be inferior to the other socially, the constitution of the United States cannot put them upon the same plane,"[7] the ruling found.

In *Plessy v. Ferguson* the Supreme Court defended the right of states to pass laws segregating the races as long as facilities were provided for both races. Although the phrase *separate but equal* was mentioned nowhere in the decision, this became the foundation on which states and cities based segregation laws.

The only judge to vote against this majority opinion was John Harlan, who wrote, "Our Constitution is color-blind, and neither knows nor tolerates classes among citizens. In respect of civil rights, all citizens are equal before the law."[8] Harlan also worried about what the court's ruling would mean for the future:

The present decision . . . will not only stimulate aggressions, more or less brutal and irritating, upon the admitted rights of colored citizens, but will encourage the belief that it is possible, by means of state enactments, to defeat the beneficent purposes which the people of the United States had in view when they adopted the recent [Thirteenth and Fourteenth] amendments of the Constitution.[9]

Jim Crow Laws Gain Momentum

The Supreme Court's ruling provided impetus for states to pass a plethora of new Jim Crow laws mandating separate public facilities for blacks and whites. "Only three states had required or authorized the Jim Crow waiting room in railway stations before 1899, but in the next decade nearly all of the other Southern states fell in line,"[10] writes historian C. Vann Woodward. State and local governments throughout the South soon passed laws requiring segregation on streetcars and steamboats, in hospitals and schools, at movie theaters and public parks. Louisiana passed legislation requiring separate entrances, exits, ticket windows, and ticket sellers at circus and tent shows. The city of Birmingham, Alabama, applied the principle to "any room, hall, theatre, picture house, auditorium, yard, court, ball park, or other indoor or outdoor place."[11] Some states required segregated workrooms in factories and businesses and forbade blacks and whites from using the same doorways, stairways, or pay windows at the same time. A South Carolina law even dictated that blacks and whites had to look out of different windows during their breaks. Where laws did not exist, private establishments set up their own rules whereby the races were prohibited from interacting at any time.

A young black teacher reads to his students in a segregated Virginia school in the 1940s. Many jobs were closed to blacks but teaching in an all-black school was one of the few good jobs open to African Americans in the South during the Jim Crow era.

By the mid-1900s Jim Crow was entrenched throughout the South. In *Plessy v. Ferguson* the Supreme Court had ruled that it was legal to provide separate but equal facilities for blacks and whites. In reality, however, the facilities for blacks were almost uniformly inferior to those for whites. Public facilities for African Americans were inconvenient, unsanitary, and often unsafe. Vincent Harding, in his prologue to the *Eyes on the Prize Civil Rights Reader*, writes that there were "two sets of doors, two kinds of facilities, from ticket line to water fountains, from waiting rooms to public schools. One white, one colored, one reasonably clean, well cared for, well supplied, the other usually broken, neglected by the white authorities, shamefully unequal."[12]

Private businesses were under no obligation to serve blacks at all. Throughout the South—and in many other parts of the country—African Americans were denied rooms at hotels, food in restaurants, and entrance to public parks, beaches, or pools simply because of the color of their skin. Stores did not allow blacks to try on clothes before buying them and often had bathrooms only for whites. When a restroom was available for blacks, it was sometimes a shared facility for both women and men. Often it was a crowded and unsanitary facility that the janitor never bothered to clean.

White southerners thought of themselves as racially superior and considered segregation laws to be following the natural order of things. Many blacks, adults and children alike, accepted this view of their place in southern society. In *A Dream of Freedom*, author Diane McWhorter writes, "For a black or white child growing up [in the South] before 1964, the most tragic thing about this segregated world was that eventually it would start to feel normal."[13]

Education and Jobs

Getting a good education was all but impossible for most African Americans. Schools for blacks were grossly underfunded. Some were depressing buildings with broken windows, peeling paint, and inadequate heating and bathroom facilities. When things broke, repairs were slow. Teachers and students often lacked books and other basic teaching materials. In some states the school year for blacks was considerably shorter than for whites. Many of the teachers at the African American schools had grown up in the South where they themselves had gotten an inadequate education.

In many communities, teaching at a black school was one of the few professions open to African Americans. Trade unions denied membership to blacks, and private businesses refused to hire them. The difficulty in getting a basic education meant becoming a doctor, dentist, or lawyer was an unrealistic goal for most African Americans. The few who succeeded in securing these professions almost always served only the black community. In the 1950s as before, African Americans worked in the only jobs they could get—mostly low-paying menial jobs. Even during the economic boom following World War II, African Americans found it difficult to get ahead. "We were the last to be hired and the first to be fired,"[14] writes Ralph Abernathy, an Alabama minister and civil rights leader.

Disenfranchisement

If African Americans had little economic power following World War II, they had even less political power. Throughout the South, states found ways to get around the Fifteenth Amendment, which said that "governments in the United States may not prevent a citizen from voting because of his race, color, or previous condition of servitude." One common strategy was the implementation of a poll tax. In some states the poll tax was assessed not just for the current year but for all years since the registrant had been eligible to vote. Since most blacks had little or no money following the Civil War, this prohibited all but a very few from voting. It was, in the opinion of one observer at the time, "the most effective bar to Negro suffrage ever devised."[15] Alabama's poll tax proved to be an insurmountable obstacle for an estimated 98 percent of voting-age blacks.

As blacks gained wealth, an increasing number of states passed laws requiring a literacy test as a prerequisite for voting. This put the power to vote in the hands of the person conducting the test, who could say that a black person failed even if he or she had not. Some of the literacy tests were so difficult that they were nearly impossible to pass. In addition to basic reading and writing skills, the applicant might be asked to recite the entire US Constitution or answer in-depth questions about obscure state laws. Some states also required voters to possess "good character," leaving the definition up to the registrars. Some localities used the literacy tests to exclude poor whites as well as blacks from voting; others required only blacks to take the tests or included clauses that would allow illiterate whites to vote.

Primary elections were also used to exclude black participation. Beginning with Mississippi in 1902, states passed laws declaring political parties to be private organizations, which made them exempt from

The Birth of the Ku Klux Klan

In the summer of 1865 six young ex-Confederate soldiers started a club in the small town of Pulaski, Tennessee. They called it the Ku Klux Klan. At its first official meeting in April 1867, the Klan adopted rules and established an organizational and leadership structure. Nathan Bedford Forrest, a former Confederate general, was elected to be the first "Grand Wizard." Secret handshakes and codes were used to conceal members' identities.

Some historians believe the first Klansmen donned sheets and rode out into the night as a joke, but the nightly raids soon became no joking matter. The sight of the hooded men instilled fear in those who saw them. The growing propensity for violence caused Forrest to officially disband the Klan in 1869, but many local units remained. In the early 1900s the Klan had a resurgence, due in part to growing anti-immigrant sentiment. At this time the Klan became a highly organized instrument of terror, initiating vigilante justice against African Americans, immigrants, and others. Lynching became a common weapon.

From these roots the Ku Klux Klan built its power in the 1950s and 1960s. Many Klansmen were local elected officials or police officers, meting out their own idea of justice when the laws did not support white supremacist goals. The Klan bombed churches and homes of civil rights leaders and viciously beat and murdered civil rights followers. Today, there remain an estimated five thousand Klansmen in the United States.

the requirements of the Fifteenth Amendment. The white primary prevented the small number of blacks who succeeded in registering to vote from having any say in who was elected to office at the local, state, or federal levels of government.

States included provisions in laws requiring poll taxes, literacy tests, and other voting restrictions that exempted from the requirements people whose grandfathers were allowed to vote. The so-called grandfather clause was designed to make it easy for whites to vote while restricting the vote of blacks, whose grandfathers—like them—had been denied voting rights.

Where institutional measures were not enough to keep blacks from voting, whites engaged in intimidation tactics. Blacks were at the mercy of employers, who could fire them at any time without giving a reason. Some whites used this power to keep blacks from attempting to vote, from issuing complaints of discrimination, or from pursuing other actions by which blacks might gain power. When all else failed, whites resorted to violence. On election day, whites lined the streets near voting polls, blocking the path of African Americans. Blacks who persisted in trying to vote might be beaten or killed.

Violence and Intimidation

Knowing that resistance might bring down the wrath of the white mob on one's parents, spouse, or children, few blacks stood up to these discriminatory practices. Attempting to vote was perhaps one of the more obvious offenses punished by violent groups such as the Ku Klux Klan, which expanded its membership and mission in the early 1900s. While many of its actions remained political in nature, the group used terrorist tactics to avenge what it judged as assaults on whites. Anyone who was black—adults and children alike—were at risk of being beaten or killed. Although many blacks were hauled off in the middle of the night, the Klan or other vigilante groups sometimes publicized the violence to send a message to others. Grace Hale, who studied the culture of segregation in the South in the early twentieth century, writes:

It was a world where people who went to church some days watched or participated in the torture of their neighbors on others. . . . Lynchers drove cars, spectators used cameras, out-of-town visitors arrived on specially chartered excursion trains, and the towns and counties in which these horrifying events happened had newspapers, telegraph offices, and even radio stations that announced times and locations of these upcoming violent spectacles.[16]

The justice system did little or nothing to protect blacks from such violence. Even when the authorities knew who was involved in violence against blacks, the perpetrators were rarely arrested or brought to trial. The few that were tried were almost never convicted.

Blacks, on the other hand, were often convicted of crimes even with no evidence of their guilt. One of the most famous cases involved nine

Two young African American men, lynched by a white mob, hang in the public square in Marion, Indiana, in 1930. Brutality against blacks was more prevalent in the South but existed as well in the North during this time period.

black teens in Scottsboro, Alabama, who were accused of raping two white girls in 1931. At trial, eight of the nine Scottsboro Boys, as they had become known, were found guilty by an all-white jury. The case went all the way to the US Supreme Court, which ruled that the defendants had not received a fair trial and ordered a retrial. In the subsequent trials, one of the girls recanted her story and stated that none of the boys had touched either of the girls. Despite the lack of evidence, four of the defendants were convicted of rape and sentenced to prison. The last of the Scottsboro Boys was released in 1950, after serving over a decade in prison.

Segregation as the Norm

African Americans had little choice but to accept the status quo. By the mid-1950s blacks and whites attended different schools, churches, theaters, restaurants, and even public parks. They used separate bathrooms and water fountains and rode on segregated buses and trains. While a set of strict rules governed the behavior of African Americans, confrontations between blacks and whites were not uncommon. And always present was an underlying threat of violence.

African Americans knew that even a minor act of defiance could come at great cost. But always, a courageous few would stand up for themselves and their community against injustice. Some fought in the courts, others in the halls of government; still others sought to engage the hearts and minds of their neighbors. From their example, others drew strength. On their shoulders rested the civil rights movement.

Chapter 2

The Seeds of Resistance

Some African Americans resisted laws and social norms that kept them at the bottom of the social order. Some refused to do business with segregated movie theatres, restaurants, or other businesses. Others continued to try to register to vote no matter how many times they were turned away. Some spoke out to demand their rights as human beings and as Americans. But the vast majority of African Americans, powerless economically and politically, made the best of the hand they were dealt.

Although the South became known for its racist policies, the North was not exempt from racial intolerance or violence either; as cities experienced an influx of African Americans from the South, they too passed laws to keep them separate. African Americans who fled the South in search of better living conditions in northern cities often found themselves pushed into black-only neighborhoods and menial jobs.

Legal Challenges

Following a race riot that broke out in Springfield, Illinois, in the summer of 1908, several black and white leaders came together in New York to discuss proposals for an organization that would advocate the civil and political rights of African Americans. The result was the National Association for the Advancement of Colored People (NAACP). In 1910, in the face of intensifying adversity, the NAACP began its legacy of fighting legal battles addressing social injustice. Its first defendant was Pink Franklin, a black sharecropper. Franklin had killed one of two armed policemen who had broken into his home in the middle of the night without stating their purpose, which was to arrest him on a civil charge. Although this was a clear case of self-defense, Franklin was convicted of murder and sentenced to death. The NAACP appealed to South Carolina's governor and succeeded in changing his sentence to life in prison. (Franklin was set free in 1919.)

Much of the NAACP's efforts focused on overturning the Jim Crow laws. The NAACP achieved its first major success in *Buchanan v. Worley*, a 1917 case in which the Supreme Court declared unconstitutional a Louisville, Kentucky, ordinance allowing people to sell their houses only to whites. The NAACP also focused on voting rights. In 1915 the Supreme Court outlawed the use of grandfather clauses in voting legislation, and in 1927 the all-white primary was eliminated.

The NAACP had achieved several important victories, but progress was slow. Jim Crow laws had been passed not just by states, but by local governments as well. For every Jim Crow law that it succeeded in overturning, hundreds more remained.

Early Activism

World War II brought about drastic changes in the United States and beyond American shores. Black Americans had joined the war effort and demonstrated bravery on and off the battlefield. Some African Americans began to wonder why they risked their lives to defend the rights of people abroad when they had not yet won these rights for themselves at home. Many had experienced better, more equal treatment in other parts of the world, which reinforced their resolve to win their rights in America. In the years following the war, African Americans won a series of victories. In 1945 Connecticut became the first state to ban laws requiring the races to be segregated. Just three years later, President Harry Truman issued an executive order ending segregation in the armed forces. White primaries and literacy tests were declared unconstitutional. And, thanks to the unflagging efforts of NAACP lawyers, a number of colleges and universities opened their doors to blacks for the first time.

Psychology and Segregation

In the 1940s psychologist and educator Kenneth B. Clark developed a test to measure the self-esteem of black children. He showed test subjects, ranging in ages from six to nine, a black doll and a white doll and asked them what they thought of each. More than half of the children said that the black doll looked "bad" and that the white doll looked "nice." A surprising number of the black children chose the white doll as the one that looked most like them.

Clark published his findings in a 1950 report. "These children saw themselves as inferior," he concluded, "and they accepted the inferiority as part of reality." Clark's research became an integral part of the NAACP's case in *Brown v. Board of Education* and was cited by the Supreme Court in its ruling.

Quoted in "Interview with Dr. Kenneth Clark," *Eyes on the Prize: America's Civil Rights Years (1954–1965),* PBS, November 4, 1985. http://digital.wustl.edu/e/eop/eopweb/cla0015 .0289.020drkennethclark.html.

Members of the Congress of Racial Equality (CORE), a civil rights organization founded in Chicago in 1942, decided to test some of the new laws. In 1947, following the Supreme Court's 1946 ruling outlawing racial segregation in interstate travel, sixteen men—eight white and eight black—boarded buses in Virginia and traveled for two weeks through North Carolina, Tennessee, and Kentucky. In defiance of the segregation policies of the bus systems, the black riders sat in front, the whites sat in the back, or they sat side-by-side. The riders were arrested several times, but violence was minimal. The riders forced the national government to enforce the Supreme Court's ruling over the protests of the states. The Journey of Reconciliation, as this event was called, demonstrated the benefits of direct action.

Brown v. Board of Education

In 1950 more than eleven thousand school districts, including most of the school districts in the Deep South, were segregated. In theory, the districts were meeting the separate but equal standard; in reality, they were anything but equal. In rural Clarendon County, South Carolina, white students made up only 13 percent of the public school population. Nevertheless, the county budgeted roughly $179 per student at white schools compared with $43 per student at black schools. Whites went to school in brick buildings with well-maintained facilities; the schools for blacks were small wooden structures with just one or two classrooms and no running water or electricity. The county also provided buses for white students but not for blacks. Some black students had to walk miles to get to school. Parents of black students in Clarendon County sued for equal education, but in 1951 the court ruled that the schools fell within the legal parameters of separate but equal.

Immediately following the Clarendon County ruling, the NAACP turned its attention to a case brought by thirteen black families in Topeka, Kansas. The local NAACP chapter had encouraged the African American families to enroll their children in the closest neighborhood school, regardless of whether it was integrated. Unlike the Deep South, Kansas was not strictly divided along racial lines, but its schools were segregated. Linda Brown Thompson, who was just nine when her father signed his name to the class action suit, later reminisced, "We lived in an integrated neighborhood and I had all of these playmates of different nationalities, so when I found out that . . . I might be able to go to their school, I was just thrilled."[17] But when she showed up for the first day of school, Linda—like the children of the other twelve plaintiffs in the lawsuit—was turned away.

Prior to enrolling in the neighborhood school, Linda and her sister had to walk six blocks through a dangerous railroad switchyard to catch a bus for the rest of the long distance to school. The other twelve families in *Brown et al. v. Board of Education* had similar situations. The NAACP argued that requiring students like Linda to travel much farther than other neighborhood children to attend school was inherently unequal. When the district court ruled against the plaintiffs, citing the "separate but equal" clause, the NAACP appealed to the Supreme Court.

The lawsuit in Topeka was but one of several school segregation cases that the Supreme Court was scheduled to hear. Since they all involved largely the same legal principles, the court decided to rule on them as a group. Thurgood Marshall and the other members of the NAACP legal team argued that the segregated schools did not conform to the Fourteenth Amendment's equal protection clause. The lawyers argued that the education received at black schools was inferior to that at schools for white students.

On May 17, 1954, after more than a year of legal wrangling, the Supreme Court issued its finding that segregated schools were unconstitutional. The court based its ruling on the principle that segregation by

African American soldiers man an antiaircraft battery near the front lines in Italy during World War II. Demonstrations of bravery both on and off the battlefield seemed to have had little effect at home, where blacks still had few of the rights enjoyed by other Americans.

itself was psychologically harmful to black students—even when comparable buildings and teachers existed. In the majority opinion, Chief Justice Earl Warren wrote, "We conclude that in the field of public education, the doctrine of 'separate but equal' has no place. Separate educational facilities are inherently unequal."[18]

The Little Rock Nine

Following the 1954 Supreme Court ruling in *Brown v. Board of Education*, state governments in the South looked for loopholes to keep segregation intact. In Mississippi, white citizen councils formed to keep black people out of white neighborhoods so that their children would not have to attend the same schools. Some African Americans who feared for the safety of their children also sought to segregate themselves in order to stay at all-black schools. The schools argued before the Supreme Court that the task of desegregation was too onerous. In a decision that became known as *Brown II*, the Supreme Court ruled that district courts should ensure that the schools be integrated "with all deliberate speed."[19] The interpretation of this phrase was left to the district courts; consequently, the states and school districts used this opportunity to continue to drag out the process.

The NAACP encouraged African Americans to take advantage of the Supreme Court decision by registering at the newly integrated schools. In Little Rock, Arkansas, the NAACP helped nine black students to register at the previously all-white Central High School, which the Little Rock School Board had voted to integrate beginning in the 1957 school year.

The decision to integrate Little Rock's schools was highly unpopular among many white residents. Some whites vowed to go to the school to physically block the black students from entering. Hoping to win white support in the upcoming gubernatorial election, Governor Orval Faubus sent National Guard troops to Central High School on the first day of school to stop the black students from entering the building. When the students arrived, they met an angry mob of whites who hurled insults and shouted at them to go home. Elizabeth Eckford, a fifteen-year-old black student who had arrived at the high school alone, later described her experience:

> When I was able to steady my knees, I walked up to [a] guard who had let white students in. . . . When I tried to squeeze past him, he raised his bayonet and then the other guards closed in and they raised their bayonets. They glared at me with a mean look and I was very frightened and didn't know what to do. I turned around and the crowd came toward me. They moved closer and closer. Somebody started yelling, "Lynch her! Lynch her!"
>
> I tried to see a friendly face somewhere in the mob—someone who maybe would help. I looked into the face of an old woman and it seemed a kind face, but when I looked at her again, she spat on me. They came closer, shouting, "No nigger bitch is going to get in our school. Get out of here!"[20]

The plight of the students attracted the attention of national media. Thousands of viewers tuned into the nightly news to witness the standoff between armed guards and the students who had become known as the "Little Rock Nine."

The situation also attracted the attention of the federal government. For several weeks, President Dwight D. Eisenhower tried to reason with Faubus. When it became increasingly evident that the state was intent on ignoring federal law, Eisenhower took action. On September 24 Eisenhower assumed control of the Arkansas National Guard, which would later be assigned to protect the nine African American students. The next day, protected by armed troops, the Little Rock Nine stepped through the doors of their new high school for the first time.

Rosa Parks

The legal victory in *Brown v. Board of Education* and the integration of previously all-white schools spurred others to challenge segregation laws in other cities and establishments. On December 1, 1955, after a long day of work as a seamstress in Montgomery, Alabama, Rosa Parks prepared to take the bus home as always. When the bus arrived at her stop, she stepped up the stairs and plunked a dime into the fare box. Then, as the custom of the day dictated, Parks stepped back off the bus and reentered by the rear door so she would not walk through the section reserved for whites. The bus was crowded, but she found a seat on the aisle a few rows from the back.

Two stops later, all of the seats in the whites-only section at the front of the bus were taken, leaving a white man standing in the aisle. The bus driver asked the four people in Parks's row to stand to allow the man to sit. The man sitting between Parks and the window stood up and squeezed past her to stand in the aisle. The two women across the aisle also stood. But Parks kept her seat. She was already seated behind the line segregating black from white passengers, and she did not think she should have to move. She knew she might be asking for trouble, but she wanted to stand up for what she thought was her right—and the right of other African Americans. "People always say that I didn't give up my seat because I was tired, but that isn't true," Parks later said. "I was not tired physically, or no more tired than I usually was at the end of a working day. . . . No, the only tired I was, was tired of giving in."[21]

When Parks was arrested, the African American community was ready. Black civil rights leaders in Montgomery had been looking for a test case to take to court, and Park's seemed to fit the bill. She had long been an active member of the NAACP and was the secretary of its local chapter in Montgomery. In addition, Parks had not violated any segregation laws. She was not sitting in the seats reserved for whites. The law required blacks to relinquish their seats only if seats were available further toward the rear of the bus. Although this was the official policy, in practice, drivers typically ordered blacks to give up their seats to white riders even if that meant standing in the aisle.

Bus Boycotts

As lawyers prepared to defend Parks in court, activists sought to hit the city where it hurt—by boycotting the bus system. In 1953, the African American community in Baton Rouge, Louisiana, where an es-

Rosa Parks is fingerprinted after her 1956 arrest for participating in the bus boycott in Montgomery, Alabama. Shortly before this time, Parks had become well known for her refusal to give up her seat to a white bus passenger.

timated 80 percent of the riders were black, had staged a boycott of city buses. Louisiana state law required buses to reserve at least the front ten rows for white passengers, a practice that seemed to some people to be not only unfair but outright absurd. Reverend T.J. Jemison, who was among the leaders of the Baton Rouge boycott, remembers seeing city buses with blacks standing in crowded aisles at the back of the bus, while in the front were rows of empty seats. "I thought that was just out of order," he says. "That was just cruel."[22]

Jemison called together leaders of the African American community to plan a boycott of the buses. The response was overwhelming. African Americans stayed off the buses, which were almost empty as they continued their routes through the city. Car pools were arranged

Gandhi and the Principles of Nonviolent Resistance

Many of the African Americans who led the civil rights movement in the 1950s and 1960s looked to Mohandas Gandhi for inspiration. Gandhi was born in 1869 in British-controlled India. After studying law in London, Gandhi went to South Africa in 1893. About a week after arriving, Gandhi's work took him from Durban to Pretoria. He bought a first-class ticket, but when the train reached Maritzburg, the capital of Natal, railroad officials ordered him to a second-class compartment because of his dark skin color. When Gandhi refused to move, the police threw him and his luggage off the train, which left without him.

This event set the course for the rest of Gandhi's life. He spent the next twenty-one years in South Africa opposing laws that discriminated against Indians, known at the time as *coloreds*, living there. He pioneered the use of mass nonviolent civil disobedience as a form of protest. He called his campaign *satyagraha*, a combination of two words meaning truth and force.

In 1914 Gandhi returned to India and introduced the methods of *satyagraha.* His ultimate goal was independent self-rule for India, but he championed more moderate causes along the way, including the alleviation of poverty of farmers and laborers, women's rights, and an end to the caste system. After decades of struggle, India gained its independence from Britain in 1947.

to help people get where they needed to go. After eight days, the city council agreed to a compromise in which the front two seats would be for whites and the back two for black riders. The rest of the seats would be filled in from that point, with white passengers taking seats at the front and moving toward the back, and blacks taking the seats furthest back and moving forward.

The impact of the bus boycott in Baton Rouge went beyond the new policy; the boycott proved that Jim Crow laws could be challenged successfully through mass action. Activists in Montgomery believed that a boycott of that city's buses could bring about change as well. These early activists stopped short of demanding an end to segregation. Rather, they asked for more subtle changes: to allow African Americans to remain in their seats in the black section of the bus or to make more seats available for blacks. They also suggested that the bus company change the policy requiring blacks to step back off the bus after paying to reboard at the rear—a policy that sometimes resulted in a paying customer being left at the curb.

From the beginning, participation in the Montgomery Bus Boycott surpassed all expectations. December 5, 1955, the day the boycott was scheduled to begin, was cold and overcast; organizers worried that the weather would break the resolve of the African American community to boycott the buses. But their worries proved unfounded: bus after bus rolled by without a single black rider and with only a few white passengers. "We surprised ourselves," one of the leaders of the boycott later said. "Never before had black people demonstrated so clearly how much those city buses depended on their business. More important, never before had the black community of Montgomery united in protest against segregation on the buses."[23]

Martin Luther King Jr.

Among the leaders of the boycott was a twenty-six-year-old Baptist minister, Martin Luther King Jr. He was new to Montgomery, but he had already become known for his oratory skills. King was tapped to lead the boycott.

At mass meetings of African Americans, King explained the rationale behind the boycott. He emphasized the importance of avoiding violence and advocated civil disobedience, which Mohandas Gandhi had proved to be effective in winning India's independence from British rule. "The only weapon that we have in our hands . . . is the weapon of protest," he told the boycotters at the first mass meeting. "There will be no white persons pulled out of their homes and taken out on some distant road and murdered. There will be nobody among us who will stand up and defy the Constitution. . . . We are going to have a real protest. We are going to keep walking."[24]

And keep walking they did. Through the hottest summer days and the coldest winter nights, Montgomery's African Americans chose to walk rather than take the bus. In Baton Rouge, the boycott was called off after eight days; Montgomery's boycott lasted for over a year. Gussie Nesbitt, a participant in the boycott, remembers her resolve to continue until the boycott had achieved its aims: "I walked because I wanted everything to be better for us. . . . I wanted to be one of them that tried to make it better. I didn't want somebody else to make it better for me. I walked. I never attempted to take the bus. Never. I was tired, but I didn't have no desire to get on the bus."[25]

As they had in the past, some white southerners responded with violence. They tried to intimidate the boycotters and targeted their leaders for violence. When a bomb exploded on the Kings' porch on January 30, 1956, King calmed the angry crowd that had gathered outside his house. "He who lives by the sword will perish by the sword," he cautioned. "We must love our white brothers no matter what they do to us. We must meet hate with love. What we are doing is just, and God is with us."[26]

During the long boycott, NAACP lawyers worked against segregation in the courts. On November 13, 1956, the US Supreme Court found Montgomery's bus segregation laws to be illegal, a decision that would take effect on December 20, 1956. The African American community came together to celebrate. "We had won self-respect," says Jo Ann Robinson, who had helped organize the boycott. "We had won a feeling that we had achieved, had accomplished. We felt that we were somebody, that somebody had to listen to us, that we had forced the white man to give what we knew was part of our own citizenship."[27] The next day, blacks in Montgomery returned to the city buses. The boycott had lasted 381 days.

The Power of Nonviolent Resistance

The Montgomery bus boycott signaled the beginning of a mass movement of nonviolent resistance that continued through the 1960s. Robert Graetz, a white minister in Montgomery who had supported the bus boycott, looks back on its impact: "The bus boycott was the beginning of the modern civil rights movement. Once the boycott started here, it spread to other cities. It encouraged people to get involved in other ways in dealing with other aspects of segregation and discrimination."[28]

The success of the boycott showed that African Americans could make a difference if they presented a united front and did not back down in the face of legal obstacles, intimidation, and even violence. Its strength lay in the fact that it was a grassroots effort. Local leaders repeatedly held mass meetings and reached out to the wider black community to make decisions. Nonviolent resistance, as preached by King, became an important strategy by which blacks would win their rights, one establishment, one neighborhood, and one city at a time.

Chapter 3

The Movement Organizes

As the years went on, the civil rights movement transitioned gradually from a series of isolated incidents to a nationwide system of solidarity. Churches often served as the center of the African American community, and ministers continued to play an important leadership role. New organizations also formed specifically to take on civil rights issues. Local grassroots organizations, fraternal societies, and black-owned businesses mobilized volunteers by the thousands to participate in broad-based actions planned and organized by these new national entities.

New Civil Rights Organizations Grow

Civil rights leaders came together in 1957 to form an organization that would employ the nonviolent tactics of the Montgomery bus boycott in other parts of the South. Martin Luther King Jr., Fred Shuttlesworth, and Ralph Abernathy were among the first leaders of the group that called itself the Southern Christian Leadership Conference (SCLC). The SCLC reached out to churches and community organizations. Within a few months, the group had established an office in Atlanta and expanded its mission beyond bus segregation to include other Jim Crow laws and racist practices.

In 1960 the SCLC brought together 126 young activists at Shaw University, a black university in Raleigh, North Carolina. From this meeting came the Student Nonviolent Coordinating Committee (SNCC), a student-run organization that was influential in mobilizing college students in the fight for civil rights. The SNCC staged rallies and protests in which young whites and blacks joined together to challenge segregation.

Sit-Ins

On February 1, 1960, four black college students sat at the all-white lunch counter at a Woolworth's store in Greensboro, North Carolina. When the students politely ordered coffee and doughnuts, the white server behind the counter asked them to leave. Like most lunch counters in stores throughout the South, the Greensboro Woolworth's did not serve black customers. For five hours—until the store closed—the students remained seated at the counter.

The next day, these four students returned to Woolworth's, accompanied by about twenty others. Again, they ordered food and continued to sit at the counter long after it was clear that they would not be served. More protesters came with them the following day. By the end of the week, hundreds of people crowded into the area to join the sit-in.

In the weeks that followed, sit-ins were staged in other southern cities. Whites sometimes joined the black protesters at the lunch counters and restaurant tables. Following the tactics of nonviolent resistance, the protesters sat quietly but resolutely until they were either served their food or arrested for violating segregation laws. Far from dissuading the protesters, going to jail became a symbol of pride. In a few cases, the sit-ins encouraged a business to change its policy, but in others it succeeded in doing far more: it galvanized support for the civil rights cause among smart, eager college students and gave them a way to show their support. It also helped generate sympathy in living rooms across America, as Americans watched on their television sets scenes of college students being arrested as they sat peacefully at restaurants across the South.

Freedom Rides

When the organizers of these sit-ins needed advice, they looked to the Congress of Racial Equality (CORE) for guidance. In the 1960 case *Boynton v. Virginia*, the Supreme Court prohibited laws of segregation in bus and rail stations used for interstate travel. CORE decided to test the law using tactics similar to those it had used twenty years earlier in the Journey of Reconciliation. CORE called its new effort the Freedom Rides.

On May 4, 1961, the first thirteen freedom riders—seven black and six white—left Washington, DC, on two public buses headed south. The men and women consciously defied the customs of the day: Whites selected seats at the back of the bus, while black riders sat up front. Whenever they stopped at a bus terminal, whites congregated in the areas designated for blacks, while the blacks headed for whites-only waiting areas. White southerners said the freedom riders were simply looking for trouble—and trouble they found.

As they headed southward, the harassment began. An African American rider was arrested for asking for a shoeshine in a segregated area of a bus station in Charlotte, North Carolina. Two African Americans were struck over the head as they walked toward a "Whites Only" sign at the Greyhound terminal in Rock Hill, South Carolina. On May 14, one of the buses was set on fire outside the small town of Anis-

Black smoke pours from a Freedom Rider bus set on fire in May 1961 just outside of Aniston, Alabama. A white mob tried to prevent the passengers from escaping and then attacked them as they scrambled out the windows.

ton, Alabama. A mob of whites surrounded the bus and held the doors closed to block escape. When the passengers scrambled through the windows, the crowd descended on them. The freedom riders probably would have been killed, but the violence was put to an end by a highway patrolman who happened to pass by.

The second bus made it to Birmingham, but once there, a mob of whites viciously attacked the riders with pipes and baseball bats as local police looked on. When Alabama's governor refused to provide protection for the freedom riders, CORE decided it had no choice but to evacuate the volunteers. Fearing for their safety, CORE flew them out of Birmingham to New Orleans. They were accompanied on the flight by federal troops, who were sent along for protection.

Going On

Civil rights leaders were worried that allowing the violence to put an end to the Freedom Rides would send the wrong message. Supported by the SNCC, new volunteers took the place of those who had been wounded and evacuated. For the rest of the summer, the Freedom Rides continued to crisscross the South, and white mobs continued to threaten and carry out violence against them. When riders were arrested, injured, or intimidated into quitting, new riders took their seats. By the end of the summer, more than four hundred people had participated in the Freedom Rides. Countless others had showed support by ignoring "whites only" or "colored only" signs posted at airports, train stations, and other transportation facilities.

The freedom riders accomplished their objective. They showed the world that state governments planned to ignore the Supreme Court's ruling in *Boynton v. Virginia*—and any other rulings that went against the Jim Crow system. The riders pushed President Kennedy to intercede on behalf of African Americans. On September 22, 1961, the Interstate Commerce Commission issued new rules for desegregation of transportation facilities. One by one, the signs came down.

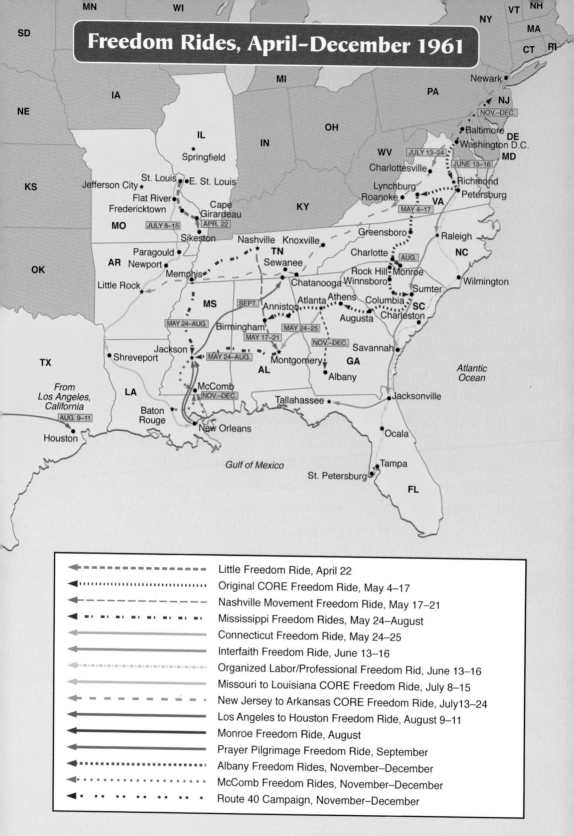

Freedom Rides, April–December 1961

Little Freedom Ride, April 22
Original CORE Freedom Ride, May 4–17
Nashville Movement Freedom Ride, May 17–21
Mississippi Freedom Rides, May 24–August
Connecticut Freedom Ride, May 24–25
Interfaith Freedom Ride, June 13–16
Organized Labor/Professional Freedom Rid, June 13–16
Missouri to Louisiana CORE Freedom Ride, July 8–15
New Jersey to Arkansas CORE Freedom Ride, July13–24
Los Angeles to Houston Freedom Ride, August 9–11
Monroe Freedom Ride, August
Prayer Pilgrimage Freedom Ride, September
Albany Freedom Rides, November–December
McComb Freedom Rides, November–December
Route 40 Campaign, November–December

Steps Toward Integration

As activists demonstrated the need for the federal government to enforce antisegregation laws, the NAACP continued to hammer away at laws that denied equal opportunities to African Americans. In 1961 James Meredith, an African American student at Jackson State College, applied to the University of Mississippi. His application was rejected several times, prompting Meredith to file a complaint that he had been denied admission because of his race. Backed by the NAACP, Meredith won his case on appeal and prepared to become the first black enrollee in the fall of 1962.

Among the many Mississippians who planned to stop Meredith was Mississippi governor Ross Barnett. Even after the Supreme Court had upheld the ruling in Meredith's favor, Barnett defended segregation. In a television broadcast, he promised that Mississippi would "not surrender to the evil and illegal forces of tyranny . . . no school will be integrated in Mississippi while I am governor."[29] He promised to bar Meredith from Ole Miss "by force, if necessary."[30]

President Kennedy and his brother Robert, the US attorney general, made a series of phone calls in an attempt to reason with Barnett. "A lot of states haven't had the guts to take a stand," Barnett told the attorney general. "We're going to fight this thing."[31]

After weeks of wrangling, Barnett agreed to allow federal marshals to stand guard in front of the campus's main building where Meredith was to register. They were joined by state troopers. Barnett issued a statement announcing that state law enforcement officers had orders to prevent any disturbances, but defiant to the end, Barnett added, "To the officials of the federal government, I say: Gentlemen, you are trampling on the sovereignty of this great state and depriving it of every vestige of honor and respect as a member of the Union of States. You are destroying the Constitution of this great nation."[32]

On the afternoon of October 1, 1962, a crowd gathered on the campus and called for the marshals to be removed. They began throwing rocks and bottles at the marshals. The state police did little at first, then withdrew as the crowd became more unruly. By 8:00 p.m. some twenty-five hundred people had converged on campus, some of whom were armed with iron pipes, rifles, and other weapons. The marshals had instructions not to fire and tried to defend themselves with tear gas, the only weapon they were allowed to use. President Kennedy was concerned about the marshals, but he also worried that the mob would find and kill Meredith. When it became clear the state was not going to come to the aid of the marshals, Kennedy called in the army. By the time the troops arrived in the wee hours of the morning, 160 federal marshals had been injured, 28 by bullet wounds. A French journalist on assignment for a London newspaper and a local resident were killed in the melee.

The next day, federal troops protected Meredith as he became the first black man to register at the University of Mississippi. He later summed up the events: "I had accomplished my goal of forcing the federal government to use the U.S. military to assert my rights as a citizen."[33]

Showdown at the University of Alabama

A similar confrontation occurred just a year later when the court ordered the University of Alabama to admit two African American students, James Hood and Vivian Malone. Kennedy had learned from his experience that segregation might not come easily, particularly given Governor George Wallace's steadfast opinion on segregation. In his 1963 inaugural speech, Wallace had said, "In the name of the greatest people that have ever trod this earth, I draw the line in the dust and toss the gauntlet before the feet of tyranny . . . and I say . . . segregation now . . . Segregation tomorrow . . . Segregation forever!"[34]

Wallace had come to power on a platform that promised whites the continuation of segregation, and Kennedy had expected his opposition. He sent deputy attorney general Nicholas Katzenbach to accompany the students to registration. When they arrived, Wallace stood in front of the door of the school's auditorium, blocking the path to the registration clerks. When Katzenbach approached, Wallace read a prepared statement calling the federal government's intervention "unwelcomed, unwanted, unwarranted, and force-induced." Wallace added,

Letter from a Birmingham Jail

The Birmingham campaign was not universally accepted by African Americans, many of whom believed that the methods were unnecessarily confrontational. On April 12, 1963, a group of eight white church leaders from Birmingham appealed to "both our white and Negro citizenry to observe the principles of law and order and common sense." The authors argued that disagreements should be resolved by the courts, not by demonstrations "directed and led in part by outsiders" which they argued were "unwise and untimely."

On April 16, King responded from jail with a lengthy letter that rebutted the arguments.

> One of the basic points in your statement is that the action that I and my associates have taken in Birmingham is untimely. . . . Frankly, I have yet to engage in a direct-action campaign that was "well timed" in the view of those who have not suffered unduly from the disease of segregation. For years now I have heard the word "Wait!" It rings in the ear of every Negro with piercing familiarity. This "Wait" has almost always meant "Never." . . . We have waited for more than 340 years for our constitutional and God-given rights.

"Statement by Alabama Clergymen," April 12, 1963, www.stanford.edu.

Martin Luther King Jr., "Letter from Birmingham Jail," April 16, 1963. http://mlk-kpp01.stanford.edu.

"I stand here today, as Governor of this sovereign state, and refuse to willingly submit to illegal usurpation of power by the Central Government." When Katzenbach asked Wallace to step aside, Wallace defiantly remained in the doorway. "I stand according to my statement,"[35] he said. Katzenbach assured the governor that the federal government was prepared to enforce the court's order. He declared, "The students will remain on this campus. They will register today. They will go to school tomorrow."[36]

When Katzenbach telephoned Kennedy with a report of what had occurred, the president federalized Alabama's National Guard. That afternoon, an officer of the National Guard informed Wallace, "It is my sad duty to ask you to step aside, on order of the President of the United States."[37] As Wallace left, a guard at the top of the auditorium raised a white flag of surrender. The University of Alabama had become the last state university in the country to desegregate.

Birmingham Campaign

Birmingham, Alabama, was among the most segregated cities in the nation. Local laws required segregation for "any room, hall, theatre, picture house, auditorium, yard, court, ball park, or other indoor or outdoor place."[38] In the summer of 1961, freedom riders had met in Birmingham some of the most aggressive and violent opposition to their attempts to test federal laws requiring desegregation. For these reasons, Shuttlesworth convinced the other leaders of the SCLC to target Birmingham for the next stage of the war on segregation.

The SCLC saw Birmingham as an opportunity. The group's leaders hoped that a mix of nonviolent boycotts, sit-ins, and demonstrations would provoke a strong response from city leaders, which would in turn ignite public interest. Wyatt Tee Walker, who planned the Birmingham campaign, explains, "My theory was that if we mounted a strong nonviolent movement, the opposition would surely do something to attract the media, and in turn induce national sympathy and attention to the everyday segregated circumstance of a person living in the Deep South."[39]

Medgar Evers: A Mississippi Martyr

In 1954 Medgar Evers, a World War II veteran and college graduate, became the first full-time NAACP field worker in Mississippi. In this role, he worked tirelessly on behalf of African Americans. He lent his support to victims of racial violence and helped bring Emmett Till's murder to light. In 1962 he helped James Meredith become the first student to attend the University of Mississippi.

Evers was a frequent target of white supremacists who saw their power slipping away. In May 1963 a bomb was thrown at his home; a month later, he narrowly escaped being run down by a car as he walked from his NAACP office to his car.

On June 11, 1963, Evers stayed late at work to watch President Kennedy deliver an impassioned speech in support of national civil rights legislation. Evers then attended a meeting with NAACP lawyers before heading home. When he arrived in his carport, Byron de la Beckwith, a member of the White Citizens Council, stepped from behind a bush and shot Evers in the back with a rifle. Evers died at the hospital an hour later.

The evidence against Beckwith was overwhelming, but, as with Emmett Till's murder eight years earlier, justice was a long time coming. The all-white jury who heard the case deadlocked, allowing Beckwith to go free. He was finally convicted of the first-degree murder of Medgar Evers in 1994.

The campaign began with a boycott of Birmingham's businesses. The next phase—Project Confrontation, or Project C for short—was a series of well-orchestrated sit-ins at white lunch counters and city libraries, kneel-ins at white churches, and street demonstrations. Public safety commissioner Eugene "Bull" Connor obtained an injunction barring the demonstrations. On April 12, 1963, fifty people, including King, Shuttlesworth, and Abernathy, were arrested for ignoring the injunction.

The Children's Crusade

As a national leader, King made news whenever he was arrested. The organizers of Project C wanted to capitalize on the national media attention, but enthusiasm for the demonstrations was beginning to wane. James Bevel, SCLC's director of direct action, introduced the idea of putting children at the head of the fight. On May 2, hundreds of black children skipped school and met at the Sixteenth Street Baptist Church. There, they were given their marching orders: groups of children would go downtown and plant themselves in segregated buildings until they were arrested. By the end of the day, Birmingham's jails overflowed with more than six hundred children, the youngest just six years old.

The next day the children were back at it. In fact, twice as many children participated, singing freedom songs as they marched downtown. Recognizing that the arrests were not having the desired impact, Connor ordered the fire department to use fire hoses to disperse the children. The full force of the water pressure sent children flying head over heels, knocked teens to their knees, and plastered adults against the walls of buildings. When the demonstrators began to throw rocks at the police, Connor called out the city's police dogs. One of the German shepherds bit a man on the leg; another dog knocked over a seven-year-old.

National TV news stations caught it all on camera: the fire hoses, the police clubs, the dogs. The brutality of the police stood in sharp contrast to the nonviolent actions of the activists. One picture seemed to sum up the horror of the events in Birmingham: Newspapers across America ran the story with a photograph showing a police dog attacking an unarmed fifteen-year-old named Walter Gadsden.

Amid public outrage, President Kennedy sent the head of the Justice Department's Civil Rights Division to work with Birmingham's leaders to reach a compromise. The gains were modest but dramatic.

Under orders from the public safety commissioner, firefighters spray black civil rights demonstrators with the full force of their fire hoses in May 1963 in Birmingham, Alabama. The brutality of the police and firefighters stood in sharp contrast to the nonviolent actions of the protesters.

On May 10 the business community agreed to end segregation and discriminatory hiring practices. The city agreed to release the protesters still in jail. Shuttlesworth said of the success: "The city of Birmingham has reached an accord with its conscience. The acceptance of responsibility by local white and Negro leadership offers an example of a free people uniting to meet and solve their problems."[40]

The March on Washington

The media coverage of police actions in Birmingham brought the civil rights movement into living rooms across America. In the months to follow, dozens of demonstrations were organized across the country from New York to California. To capitalize on the momentum, six civil rights leaders—representing the most prominent civil rights organizations of the day—came together to plan a spectacular event: a march on the nation's capital. The stated objectives of the march were to secure federal civil rights legislation, to eliminate segregation in public schools, and to protect the rights of peaceful demonstrators. The march also took up economic goals, advocating the passage of a law that would prohibit racial discrimination in hiring and establish a new minimum wage.

On August 28, 1963, about 250,000 people marched from the Washington Monument to the Lincoln Memorial. The marchers were mostly black, but about a fourth were white. Some held signs outlining their demands, such as "We march for jobs for all now!" "We demand voting rights now!" and "End segregated rules in public schools."

Some leaders worried that the event might incite violence, but as the day wore on the atmosphere became jubilant. Popular musicians such as Marian Anderson, Joan Baez, Bob Dylan, and others performed in support of the protests. Actor Charlton Heston read a speech by African American author James Baldwin. John Lewis, the SNCC representative who had been among the first freedom riders, urged the demonstrators to continue to fight injustice: "The revolution is at hand, and we must free ourselves of the chains of political and economic slavery," he said. "We cannot be patient, we do not want to be free gradually, we want our freedom, and we want it now."[41]

But the most memorable speech was the last of the day: King's "I Have a Dream Speech." King had begun with prepared notes in which he said that they had come to "cash a check" for their rights. Sensing the enthusiasm of the crowd, he set aside his speech to build on the theme that he had preached many times before, outlining his dream for America. He concluded:

And when we allow freedom to ring, when we let it ring from every village and every hamlet, from every state and every city, we will be able to speed up that day when all of God's children, black men and white men, Jews and Gentiles, Protestants and Catholics, will be able to join hands and sing in the words of the old Negro spiritual, "Free at last, free at last. Thank God Almighty, we are free at last."[42]

King's words resonated with the crowd. The march toward freedom had already taken many years, and it would take many years more. But on August 28, 1963, these African Americans—many for the first time—felt that freedom was within their grasp.

Chapter 4

The Struggle Intensifies

As African Americans organized to gain their civil rights, white supremacists organized to counter their efforts. Often with help from police and other authorities, the Ku Klux Klan orchestrated massive, violent, and sometimes deadly events to deter African Americans and their white supporters from participating in the civil rights movement. In response, new civil rights leaders emerged, arguing that the time had come for blacks to fight back and claim the rights due to them by any means necessary. The civil rights movement had become war.

Klan Violence

On Sunday, September 15, 1963, just a month after the March on Washington, a deafening blast ripped through Birmingham's Sixteenth Street Baptist Church. The church had been used as a gathering spot for demonstrators, but Sundays were reserved for worship services. On that Sunday, a bomb planted by KKK members killed four girls, ages eleven to fourteen.

The African American community was shocked by the murders, but many whites dissociated themselves from the violence. In *A Dream of Freedom*, Diane McWhorter remembers her reaction:

> I was only a year younger than Denise McNair [the youngest victim] was at the time of the church bombing, yet the murder of the four girls had no impact on me. The color line had

deprived me of the capacity to empathize with black children. . . . No one really drew a connection between our "nonviolent" bigotry and the Klan's dynamite. We [the white community] saw the church bombing as a terrible thing that had befallen an otherwise upstanding, law-abiding community.[43]

African Americans were not the only targets of white supremacist attacks; some of the most violent attacks were reserved for whites who supported civil rights. J. Res Brown, one of just four African American lawyers in Mississippi, warned volunteers from the North: "You're going to be classified into two groups in Mississippi: niggers and nigger-lovers, and they're tougher on nigger lovers."[44]

Citizens' Councils

As the tactics of the Klan became more violent, some whites seeking to maintain the status quo established more moderate organizations. These organizations, called citizens' councils, sought to find new ways around federal mandates and used their economic power to keep African Americans from participating in civil rights demonstrations or opposing the status quo. The citizens' councils included some of the most influential politicians in the South. Many business owners also joined the councils. "We were all stunned by the '54 [*Brown v. Board of Education*] decision and knew we had to preserve our culture and control our education system," says Horace Harned, a Mississippi state senator in the 1950s, in an interview. "Most people prominent in [Mississippi] politics were members of the Citizens' Council."[45]

The first citizens' council was established in Indianola, Mississippi, on July 11, 1954, just after the Supreme Court made its ruling in *Brown v. Board of Education*. By 1956 the organization had roughly eighty thousand members in chapters statewide. The citizens' councils quickly spread from Mississippi to other southern states. Newsletters and television ads stated that the goal of the councils was "to maintain peace and order of the community" to prevent "racial demonstrations"[46] from unduly influencing politicians.

Members of the citizens' councils were committed to maintaining segregation in the South. William Simmons, who founded the chapter in Jackson, Mississippi, the state's capital, said that the strategy of the citizens' councils was "to delay, to delay, to delay" any move toward desegregation by any means possible. Like most southerners who fought for segregation, Simmons believed that the federal government had no right to legislate how people in the South should live: "Why use the power of government to compel people to mix socially for the sole reason that they were of different races? There's nothing, there's no historical precedent that anyone has brought to my mind that explains this. There's no prior experience of mankind. There's plenty of the opposite, of separation, but none of this compulsion to integrate."[47]

The citizens' councils kept close tabs on civil rights activities and used their political and economic power to prevent blacks from getting involved in the movement. Council members who owned businesses fired employees suspected of sympathizing with the civil rights movement. Businesses also refused to hire black agitators or to serve anyone who had been seen at a demonstration. In Yazoo, Mississippi, a plumber who had been seen at a civil rights demonstration lost his white customers, was refused plumbing supplies by a wholesale house, and was told that he would have to pay four times the going rate for a loaf of bread. Black parents who intended to register their children at a white school might lose their jobs or be kicked out of rental homes. When fifty-three African Americans signed a petition to desegregate local schools, Yazoo banks uniformly refused to do business with them.

The citizens' councils targeted white sympathizers as well. Capitalizing on "Red Scare" fears that Communist spies were preparing to overthrow the US government, the citizens' councils spread rumors that the civil rights movement was a Communist plot. When Ed King, a Mississippi-born white who had studied at Boston University, was arrested during a sit-in, his parents were ostracized. "People stopped speaking to my mother at church, at PTA," King said. "People pushed their carts away from the aisle where she was shopping."[48]

In 1964 robed and hooded members of the Ku Klux Klan join other protesters in urging residents of Atlanta, Georgia, to boycott a restaurant that agreed to serve both black and white customers. The white citizens' councils also targeted civil rights activists—both black and white.

Freedom Summer

In the summer of 1964, known as Freedom Summer, the SNCC set its sights on registering black voters in Mississippi, which had become the front line of the war against racism. "If we can crack Mississippi," one of the leaders said, "we can crack segregation anywhere."[49]

The Kerner Commission

Following the Watts riot in 1965, widespread rioting erupted in cities across America. On June 12, 1966, rioting occurred in Chicago, Illinois, following the shooting of a Puerto Rican man by police. In Newark, New Jersey, riots and looting lasted for six days following rumors that a black cabdriver had been killed while in police custody. (The driver had, in fact, been moved to a local hospital.) On July 28, 1967, President Johnson appointed the National Advisory Commission on Civil Disorders to determine the underlying causes of these disturbances in search of a remedy.

Known as the Kerner Commission—after its chair, Illinois governor Otto Kerner Jr.—the commission issued its findings on February 29, 1968. The Kerner Report highlighted deficiencies and inequalities in housing, education, and job opportunities. The commission blamed white America for the violence in urban neighborhoods and warned, "Our nation is moving toward two societies, one black, one white—separate and unequal."

The Kerner Commission urged new legislation to promote racial integration and equality. In particular, the members focused on job creation, job training, and decent housing. Although the Kerner Report struck a chord with many Americans, black and white, the recommendations were largely ignored. One month after the report's publication, rioting broke out in more than one hundred cities following the assassination of Martin Luther King.

Quoted in "Two Societies, Separate and Unequal, 1968" in *Eyes on the Prize: America's Civil Rights Movement, 1954–1985*, PBS, www.pbs.org.

The idea behind Freedom Summer was to recruit black and white college students to help blacks register to vote in Mississippi, where intimidation, literacy tests, and other discriminatory voting requirements had resulted in extremely low rates of African American participation. In addition to registering African Americans to vote, the student volunteers set up community centers to provide legal and medical services and freedom schools to tutor children in reading and math.

The leader of the project was Bob Moses, an African American born in Harlem, New York. As field secretary for the SNCC, Moses had already had his share of near-death experiences in Mississippi. "When you're not in Mississippi, it's not real," he told the students recruited for Freedom Summer. "And when you're there, the rest of the world isn't real."[50]

Twenty-year-old Andrew Goodman was one of six hundred students who answered the call of Freedom Summer organizers. Goodman was not an experienced civil rights worker; the white college junior had lived a rather sheltered life in New York City. He felt compassion for the downtrodden, however, and wanted to make a difference.

On June 20, following training in Ohio, Goodman was paired with two other volunteers: James Chaney, a twenty-one-year-old African American from Mississippi, and Mickey Schwerner, a twenty-four-year-old white social worker from New York. The three men traveled to investigate the burning of a rural church that had been used as a freedom school—no doubt the work of the Ku Klux Klan. As they were leaving, the CORE vehicle they were driving was pulled over for speeding. The three men were held in the Philadelphia, Mississippi, jail until nightfall, when they were released to several members of the local Ku Klux Klan. They were never heard from again.

The federal government was mobilized during the search for the civil rights workers. Six weeks after they had vanished, paid informants tipped off the FBI that they were buried on a local farm. The recovery of the bodies showed that they had been beaten and shot. Seven of the eighteen men brought to trial in 1967 were found guilty, including the imperial wizard of the local Klan. Their sentences ranged from three to ten years; none of the convicted murderers served more than six.

"Although their deaths make them nationally famous and among the best known civil rights martyrs, they were among hundreds—overwhelmingly African American—who had been killed during the civil rights struggle," writes the Andrew Goodman Foundation, which was formed in the wake of their deaths to recognize and inspire civil rights activism. "But their murder, while idealistically fighting for social justice, woke up the sleeping conscience of a nation."[51]

Gaining Political Strength

If the goal of the killings was to halt the momentum behind the fight for civil rights, the strategy failed. Freedom Summer volunteers remained in Mississippi, their resolve strengthened. One of the major accomplishments of Freedom Summer was a new political party that would challenge the white-only Democratic Party in Mississippi. The Mississippi Freedom Democratic Party (MFDP) helped enable blacks to register to vote without having to stand up to whites at the courthouse or pass discriminatory literacy tests. Though it was a full-fledged political party, the MFDP was denied recognition at the 1964 Democratic National Convention—a move that deeply angered civil rights activists. John Lewis writes in his 1998 memoir:

> Until then, despite every setback and disappointment and obstacle we had faced over the years, the belief still prevailed that the system would work, the system would listen, the system would respond. Now, for the first time, we had made our way to the very center of the system. We had played by the rules, done everything we were supposed to do, had played the game exactly as required, had arrived at the doorstep and found the door slammed in our face.[52]

The convention gained national attention, but some people within the movement were distraught by the growing use of confrontation. Lewis writes, "In the wake of both Freedom Summer and of our actions at the Democratic convention, many white liberals who had previously supported us were now disturbed by our 'extreme' and 'aggressive' tactics."[53]

Bloody Sunday

SNCC and other organizations had led voter registration drives but had made little progress. As in Mississippi, state and local officials, the white citizens' council, and Ku Klux Klan in Alabama had effectively blocked blacks' attempts to vote. In Dallas County, for instance, where African Americans accounted for 57 percent of the population, less than 1 percent of blacks old enough to vote were registered. In 1965 civil rights leaders in Alabama organized a march from Selma to the state capital of Montgomery to call attention to the denial of blacks' constitutional right to vote. On March 7, the day of the planned march, about six hundred people converged in downtown Selma. Singing freedom songs, they had started to cross the Alabama River when they saw line after line of uniformed state troopers blocking the road. Many of the troopers had been deputized that morning for this purpose. The commanding officer told the marchers to go home; instead they knelt to pray. Seconds later, the troopers began to advance on the crowd, hitting protesters with clubs, poking them with cattle prods, and firing off tear gas canisters. Police on horseback charged the crowd.

Seventeen marchers were hospitalized, and many more suffered minor injuries. When the news hit the airwaves, some viewers were horrified by the televised images of the brutal attack on unarmed protesters. This incident is now remembered as "Bloody Sunday."

Malcolm X and Militancy

In the face of such adversity, a growing number of civil rights leaders believed that it was time for the African American community to take a stronger stance. In this atmosphere arose Malcolm X, a member of the Nation of Islam, an organization that called for the establishment of a separate nation for black Americans and the adoption of the Muslim religion. Malcolm X was among the most vocal advocates of a more militant approach. He urged African Americans to claim their rights "by any means necessary."[54] Articulate and intelligent, Malcolm X gained a huge following and became spokesperson for the Nation of Islam. As spokesperson, he taught that black people were superior to whites and other races and advocated the separation of blacks and whites in the United States. Malcolm X was also a vocal critic of the tactics of the mainstream civil rights movement and of King, its most well known leader. He equated nonviolence with being defenseless and called nonviolence the "philosophy of a fool."[55] He argued that blacks should fight for their rights by whatever means necessary, including taking up arms. Malcolm X told young people working in Mississippi: "I don't think it is fair to tell our people to be nonviolent unless someone is out there making the Klan and the Citizens Council and these other groups also be nonviolent. . . . You get freedom by letting your enemy know that you'll do anything to get your freedom; then you'll get it. It's the only way you'll get it."[56]

Malcolm X's radically militant views changed over time. After learning that Elijah Muhammad, the leader of the Nation of Islam, had had a series of extramarital affairs, Malcolm X publicly broke with that organization. He continued to be sought as a speaker, however, and many African Americans believed that he better expressed their sense of anger and frustration than did those who preached a path of nonviolence. On February 21, 1965, as he stepped to the podium to speak to a group of African Americans in New York City, three men rushed from the crowd and shot him. The assassins were members of the Nation of Islam; the assassination was believed to be in response to his criticism of Elijah Muhammad.

The Rise of Black Power

Like Malcolm X, Stokely Carmichael, a Howard University student who had taken part in the 1961 Freedom Rides, also became disenchanted with the slow progress of the civil rights movement. Carmichael viewed nonviolence as a tactic rather than a philosophy, and when he became head of the SNCC in 1966, he began to call for a more aggressive approach. Rather than trying to integrate African Americans into white mainstream society, Carmichael believed that the black community should unite and take pride in their race and heritage. Carmichael did not believe in asking whites for their freedom; he argued that they should *demand* it—taking it by force if need be. "No man can give anybody his freedom," said Carmichael. "A man is born free."[57]

At the center of Carmichael's philosophy was black power, which he defined as "black people coming together to form a political force and either electing representatives or forcing their representatives to speak their needs."[58] He saw the concept as a means to unite the African American community in a common goal. Black power was not a new concept, but in the mid-1960s it was embraced by a black community that was ready to take pride in its heritage and ownership of its destiny. The new catchphrase of the civil rights movement implied it was not enough to have voting rights or economic opportunities; African Americans called for black power. The concept was never clearly defined, and some adherents began to identify it with black nationalism or separatism.

Young men in Jackson, Mississippi, raise their fists in the black power salute—a symbol of a more militant approach to achieving civil rights. Members of the black power movement felt that nonviolence had achieved too little and that the time had come to demand freedom—by force, if necessary.

The Black Panters

In 1966 Huey Newton and Bobby Seale organized the Black Panther Party for Self-Defense in Oakland, California. Militant in philosophy and tactics, the Black Panthers quickly expanded into cities throughout the nation.

The Black Panthers' ten-point program "What We Want, What We Believe" combined political and economic objectives that included food, housing, education, clothing, justice, and peace. Within a couple of years, the Black Panthers in Oakland were feeding breakfast daily to more than ten thousand children before they went to school. Throughout the nation, similar community service programs were established by local Black Panther chapters.

At the forefront of the Black Panther agenda was a demand for the protection of African Americans from police brutality. The organization soon gained renown for its militant, sometimes violent, tactics, particularly in opposition to police. The Black Panthers consistently asserted their Second Amendment right to bear arms. On October 28, 1967, in an exchange of gunfire with Oakland police, Huey Newton was wounded and charged with killing a police officer. This was the first of several armed confrontations between Black Panthers and police in the ensuing years.

Once considered radical, the leaders of the NAACP and SCLC now seemed moderate in comparison. They worried about what black power meant and what it communicated to white supporters. "Racism is racism," said Roy Wilkins, the head of the NAACP. He called black power "the father of hatred and the mother of violence."[59] Still, as both a slogan and a strategy, black power caught on, suggesting that a more militant approach to the fight for civil rights was gaining momentum.

The Watts Riot

Regardless of whether they believed in black power, an increasing number of African Americans were rising up to defend their rights. The protests were not always peaceful—far from it. In some cases, the anger and fear and frustration that had built up for decades exploded into a wave of spontaneous violence. One of the most horrifying examples began on the evening of August 11, 1965, after a white highway patrolman stopped the car of twenty-one-year-old Marquette Frye in Watts, a run-down African American neighborhood of Los Angeles. The patrolman had stopped Frye on suspicion of driving while intoxicated and called for backup. When backup police arrived on the scene, a crowd gathered, including Frye's mother. Frye resisted arrest, the police attempted to use physical force to handcuff him. Frye's mother began fighting with the police; other bystanders began throwing rocks and yelling at the officers.

Frye, his mother, and his brother were arrested, but the crowd that remained behind grew increasingly unruly. Rumors wildly exaggerated details of the arrests and fabricated new offenses. Police and black community leaders met the next day, but the violence continued to escalate. For several days, rioters burned automobiles, broke windows, and looted grocery and liquor stores. Over the course of the six-day riot, roughly fifteen thousand National Guardsmen and local police were deployed. In an attempt to restore order, a curfew was imposed on a 45-square-mile (116 sq km) area. By the time the violence had ceased, thirty-four people had lost their lives and another thousand were injured. One black civil rights activist later wrote that Watts "marked the first major rebellion of Negroes against their own masochism and was carried out with the express purpose of asserting that they would no longer quietly submit to the deprivation of slum life."[60]

Black people had lost their fear. The following year, similar riots sprang up in urban centers throughout the United States, usually sparked by a minor incident. To some civil rights leaders, the riots suggested that the movement had spiraled out of control. King said, "I started seeing [my dream] turn into a nightmare."[61] To other civil rights leaders, the riots were a sign that the movement had reached to the core of the black community across the country. The civil rights movement had moved beyond the South. Los Angeles; Washington, DC; Chicago; Cleveland; Minneapolis—these were some of the hardest hit communities. Where people had once expressed their discontent through marches and demonstrations, now they expressed sheer anger in unprecedented waves of destruction. Where marches did continue, they were increasingly marred by vandalism and looting, a sign that patience had run out.

Economic Freedom

As African Americans gained legal freedoms, civil rights leaders turned their attention to gaining economic opportunities as well. Bobby Seale, a cofounder of the militant Black Panther organization, was among those who believed that racism was rooted in economic disparity. Seale called the civil rights movement "a class struggle between the massive proletarian working class and the small, minority ruling class. Working-class people of all colors must unite against the exploitative, oppressive ruling class . . . we believe our fight is a class struggle and not a race struggle."[62]

Other organizations focused their attention on addressing the poverty of African Americans. In 1967 King and the SCLC organized the Poor People's Campaign to focus on jobs, income, and housing. King believed the tactics of nonviolent resistance could be used to call attention to inequalities in the workplace, just as they had in other areas of life.

On April 4, 1968, King addressed a gathering in Memphis, where he had gone to support African American sanitation workers who had gone on strike to demand wages equal to those of whites. King's plane had been delayed on the way to Memphis because of a bomb threat. During his address to the sanitation workers he alluded to the threat:

> What would happen to me from some of our sick white brothers? Well, I don't know what will happen now. We've got some difficult days ahead. But it doesn't matter with me now. Because I've been to the mountaintop. And I don't mind. Like anybody,

I would like to live a long life. Longevity has its place. But I'm not concerned about that now. I just want to do God's will. And He's allowed me to go up to the mountain. And I've looked over. And I've *seen* the promised land."[63]

A Powerful Voice Is Silenced

That night, King stepped out onto the balcony of his hotel. He called down to invite Jesse Jackson, a new SCLC staffer, to dinner. A shot rang out, and King fell. His friends got to him within seconds, but it was too late. King, the civil rights movement's greatest speaker and most fervent advocate of nonviolence, had been silenced by an assassin's bullet.

Chapter 5

What Is the Legacy of the Civil Rights Movement?

Barack Obama was elected president of the United States in 2008, the first African American to hold the nation's highest political office. Obama's election can, in many ways, be considered the ultimate legacy of the civil rights movement. It demonstrated just how far the United States has come since the era of Jim Crow laws. In just fifty years, the nation has transitioned from keeping African Americans on the bottom of the social order to electing an African American to what some say is the most powerful position in the world. The laws that once separated black and white Americans no longer exist. Overt barriers to education have been shattered as well. Above all, Obama's election shows that the wall of racial discrimination that once separated blacks from economic and political power has crumbled.

Affirmative Action

One of the tools that gave rise to leaders like Obama is affirmative action. Decades of discriminatory practices had resulted in a class of people who, compared with their white counterparts, were undereducated, relatively unskilled, and often unprepared for the workplace. In 1961, amid the civil rights battle, President John F. Kennedy issued an executive order requiring federal contractors to "take affirmative action to ensure that applicants are employed, and that employees are treated during employment, without regard to their race, creed, color, or national origin."[64]

Kennedy introduced affirmative action as a means of redressing the discrimination faced by African Americans despite the laws and Supreme Court decisions upholding their right to equal treatment. President Lyndon B. Johnson later explained that affirmative action was part of the effort to achieve equality not just as "a right and a theory," but as "a fact and a result."[65]

Kennedy's executive order introduced a new phrase to the American lexicon, but it was not the first attempt to address discrimination

Possibly the most stunning legacy of the civil rights movement was the 2008 election of Barack Obama, the first black president of the United States. His election illustrates how far the nation and its people have come since the Jim Crow era.

in hiring. During World War II, President Franklin D. Roosevelt signed an executive order declaring "there shall be no discrimination in the employment of workers in defense industries or government because of race, creed, color, or national origin."[66] The Fair Employment Practices Committee was founded to investigate complaints and take action against cases of discrimination. The policy worked. By the end of the war, three times as many African Americans had jobs in the federal government and in the defense industry as before the war.

Affirmative action policies required that active measures be taken to ensure that African Americans enjoyed the same opportunities for school admissions, scholarships, jobs, promotions, and the like. The concept has been applied widely to educational settings, providing a rationale for looking beyond an applicant's qualifications on paper to consider the disadvantages and obstacles that an applicant has had to overcome. It has similarly been used in the hiring process. In the decades since the introduction of affirmative action, the concept has been broadened to include other people—Latinos, Native Americans, women, and people with disabilities—who may not have had the same advantages as white males.

A Controversial Practice

From the beginning affirmative action was controversial and remains so to this day. Supporters of affirmative action justify its use as essential in overcoming the circumstances of one's birth, but critics say that the concept results in discrimination against whites. In the 2003 case *Grutter v. Bollinger*, the Supreme Court upheld the right of educational institutions to consider race as a factor in admitting students. In the earlier (1978) case *Bakke v. University of California*, the Supreme Court outlawed inflexible quota systems that establish a set number of minorities to be admitted. In the workplace, affirmative action laws also require anyone benefiting from affirmative action to meet all qualifications and criteria for the job or educational opportunity.

In practice, affirmative action has helped African Americans and other minorities, particularly those who are socioeconomically disadvantaged, make strides toward equality in education and employment.

Ending the Poll Tax

One of the most widely used methods to prevent African Americans from voting was the poll tax. Poll taxes first came into use in the 1890s; by 1902 all eleven states of the former Confederacy had enacted such a tax. Poll taxes discriminated against those who could not afford to pay, but they were also used to discriminate along to racial lines. Some states required people who registered to vote to present proof that they had paid the tax for many years prior to the election—an impossible feat for African Americans who had been otherwise denied the vote. In some cases, records were kept at the sheriff's office, thereby dissuading African Americans from obtaining proof of payment. In states where all potential voters were supposed to be assessed the tax, blacks were uniformly omitted from the assessment. Despite these practices, the right of states to enact poll taxes was upheld by the Supreme Court in the 1937 ruling in *Breedlove v. Suttles*.

In addition to denying African Americans the vote, poll taxes became an instrument for election fraud. Parties paid the tax for people willing to vote for their candidate. Illegally obtained poll tax receipts were distributed by candidates to their supporters. For these and other reasons, many states did away with poll taxes. In 1964 poll taxes were outlawed in national elections with the ratification of the Twenty-Fourth Amendment. Two years later, in *Harper v. Board of Elections* (1966), the Supreme Court extended the prohibition to all elections.

Between 1974 and 1980 federal contractors that were required to adopt affirmative action goals added black and female officials at twice the rate of companies not required to adhere to affirmative action standards. According to a 1995 report from the US Labor Department, affirmative action had helped 5 million minority members move up in the workforce.

The American Problem

By the mid-1960s the civil rights movement had succeeded in bringing the nation's attention to the racial divide and its inequities. Early on, many Americans viewed the fight for civil rights as an African American problem, but the continued news coverage of injustice brought it to the forefront of the nation's consciousness. President Johnson spoke on behalf of Americans, not just black Americans, when he said: "There is no Negro problem. There is no southern problem. There is no northern problem. There is only an American problem."[67]

On the heels of President Kennedy's assassination in 1963, Johnson made civil rights legislation a priority. The result, the Civil Rights Act of 1964, became the most sweeping civil rights legislation since the Fourteenth Amendment. It bans discrimination based on race, color, religion, sex, or national origin in employment practices and nullifies state and local laws that allow discrimination. The Civil Rights Act unraveled the Jim Crow South by outlawing segregation in restaurants, theaters, hotels, and other public places. It also protects citizens' rights to equal opportunities in education and employment.

Having secured passage of the Civil Rights Act, President Johnson turned his attention to protecting voting rights. Echoing the language of the Fifteenth Amendment, the Voting Rights Act of 1965 made it illegal for states to have literacy tests, character requirements, or any other "voting qualification or prerequisite to voting, or standard, practice, or procedure" intended to deny the right to vote of any person or group of people. The act established federal oversight of elections administration. It also requires states that have a history of discriminatory voting practices (all states and voting districts in the South) to obtain the approval of the Department of Justice before making changes to their election procedures—a requirement known as preclearance. Under this requirement, a state, county, or local government must demonstrate to the federal government that the change does not have a racially discriminatory purpose and will not make minority voters worse off than they were prior to the change. Courts have applied the Voting Rights Act to end racial discrimination in state and local legislative bodies and in the choosing of poll officials.

The impact of the Voting Rights Act was almost immediate. Civil rights leaders worked aggressively to register black voters in the South.

Within months of its passage, 250,000 additional African Americans had registered to vote; by the next presidential election, voter registration in the South had doubled.

Since its passage, the Voting Rights Act has been renewed several times. In 1982 Congress strengthened the act and extended the pre-clearance requirement. In addition to protecting the rights of African Americans to vote, the legislation has served to protect the rights of other minorities, including Americans with limited English skills. The legislation requires particular jurisdictions to print ballots and other election materials in minority languages.

The Impact on Governance

At first the civil rights movement was a struggle between citizens and the laws of the state, but the federal government played an increasingly central role in the events that unfolded. The civil rights movement pitted the federal government against southern states—a stand-off that was reminiscent of events leading up to the Civil War. When states refused to enforce court rulings, the federal government stepped in. Several governors and state legislatures insisted that the federal government was exceeding its constitutional power.

In enforcing the law, federal officials became the defenders of civil rights. The Civil Rights Act of 1964, the Voting Rights Act of 1965, and other federal laws replaced state laws that had dictated segregation, and enforcement of these laws and Supreme Court rulings brought federal troops into the South for the first time since the Civil War.

The result has been a shift away from states' rights toward increasing the power of the federal government in all areas of American life. The inequities that resulted pushed the federal government to take an increasing role in legislating the way people live.

Subsequent legislation also expanded the federal government's role in enforcing nondiscriminatory practices. In April 1968, just one week after the assassination of Martin Luther King Jr., Congress passed the Fair Housing Act, which prohibits private citizens from refusing to sell or rent housing to any person because of race, color, religion, sex, or national origin.

African American Communities

The civil rights movement had a tangible impact on African American communities, not only in the South but across America. One of the unanticipated and unfortunate results of the movement was the dissolution of black communities. The civil rights movement opened up new doors for all African Americans, but some were better able to take advantage of the new opportunities than others. The Virginia Historical Society writes, "Those best able to take advantage of new opportunities were middle-class blacks—the teachers, lawyers, doctors, and other professionals who had served as role models for the black community. Their departure for formerly all-white areas left all-black neighborhoods segregated not only by race but now also by class. The problem of poverty, compounded by drugs, crime, and broken families, was not solved by the civil rights movement."[68]

Despite the many gains made by the civil rights movement, economic inequality remains. The average income of black families is significantly less than that of whites. In many parts of the country, blacks and whites continue to live in separate neighborhoods—almost always with blacks in poorer neighborhoods. As a result many schools have disparate populations, resulting in unequal opportunities for the nation's youngest residents. African Americans consistently do poorer on standardized tests, reflecting disparities in the schools they attend. Laws and affirmative action policies have helped level the playing field for African Americans, but they have not yet achieved true and complete equality.

Gaining Office

During the 1950s and 1960s, the civil rights movement was a proving ground for African American leaders. Many of the leaders of the movement took positions of leadership within the federal and state governments, where they could influence change from the inside. In 1967 Thurgood Marshall, best remembered for his role in the NAACP victory in *Brown v. Board of Education*, became the first African American on the Supreme Court. Marshall served on the court for twenty-four years, consistently and ably supporting the protection of the constitutional rights of Americans.

Equal Opportunity Is Not Enough

President Lyndon Johnson followed up on many of the ideas introduced by President Kennedy before his assassination, including affirmative action. In his 1965 commencement address at Howard University, Johnson explains the need for affirmative action:

> The barriers to that freedom are tumbling down. . . . But freedom is not enough. You do not wipe away the scars of centuries by saying, "Now you are free to go where you want, and do as you desire, and choose the leaders you please." You do not take a person who, for years, has been hobbled by chains and liberate him, bring him up to the starting line of a race and then say, "You are free to compete with all the others," and still justly believe that you have been completely fair. . . .
>
> We seek not just freedom, but opportunity. We seek not just legal equity, but human ability; not just equality as a right and a theory, but equality as a fact and equality as a result. . . .
>
> To this end, equal opportunity is essential, but not enough, not enough. Men and women of all races are born with the same range of abilities. But ability is not just the product of birth. Ability is stretched or stunted by the family that you live with and the neighborhoods you live in, by the school you go to and the poverty or the richness of your surroundings. It is the product of a hundred unseen forces playing upon the little infant, the child, and finally the man.

Lyndon B. Johnson, "Equal Opportunity Is Not Enough," Howard University Commencement Address, in *Eyes on the Prize: America's Civil Rights Movement, 1954–1985*, PBS. www.pbs.org.

Other civil rights leaders have gone on to elected positions. Andrew Young, an SCLC leader and good friend of Martin Luther King, was elected to three terms in the House of Representatives. In 1977 President Jimmy Carter appointed Young as ambassador to the United Nations; subsequently, he served two terms as mayor of Atlanta. Jesse Jackson, who served as the SCLC's national director in 1967, went on to form the Rainbow Coalition, an organization focused on securing equal rights for all Americans through social programs, voting rights, and affirmative action.

The civil rights movement forever changed politics in and beyond the South. Prior to the Voting Rights Act, only about one hundred African Americans had held elective office—and all of these were in northern states. Today, African Americans serve in important positions in all sectors of American life—from the halls of Congress, to the Supreme Court bench, to the presidency, to the board rooms of some of the biggest corporations in the nation.

Other Groups Have Benefited

While the focus of the civil rights movement was on overcoming racism and protecting the rights of African Americans, the effect has been to strengthen these rights for all people. In the Latino, or Chicano, civil rights movement, Hispanic Americans built a broad coalition to address discrimination and demand their constitutional right to equal protection under the law. The leaders of the Chicano movement joined with African American leaders in the 1968 Poor People's Campaign on Washington and used some of the tactics by which African Americans gained their rights. In 1968 the Mexican American Legal Defense and Educational Fund was formed, modeled after the NAACP Legal Defense and Educational Fund. Cesar Chavez incorporated nonviolence into the movement's core philosophy when he organized migrant workers in California.

Native American activists also borrowed tactics from the civil rights movement. In 1964 Native Americans formed an organization called the Survival of American Indians, which stages "fish-ins" to protect off-reservation fishing rights in Washington state. The American Indian Movement, founded in the summer of 1968, focuses on protecting Native Americans from police abuse and creating education, job training, and housing opportunities. In 1969 Native American groups gained publicity for their cause by taking over Alcatraz, a former prison in California.

These actions have increased tolerance on the part of the white majority while also instilling ethnic pride among the minority groups. Having gained civil rights, African Americans, Latinos, Native Americans, and others have fought to have their stories told. The experiences of minority Americans provide testimony to the concept of America as a melting pot of cultures, ideas, and philosophies. They have changed the way Americans view their past, their present, and their future.

In 1974 United Farmworkers leader Cesar Chavez (right) urges shoppers to boycott lettuce and grapes picked by nonunion farmworkers. Chavez adopted the nonviolent tactics of the civil rights movement in his work on behalf of migrant farmworkers.

Forever Changed

Although Americans have come a long way toward achieving King's dream, the effects of a racist society continue to plague the African American community. Segregated communities of all white (usually the very rich) and all black (often the very poor) neighborhoods remain. These black communities have higher rates of crime, particularly violent crime, than other parts of the country. A disproportionate number of African Americans are in prisons and on death row. All-black schools, which continue to struggle with funding and continue to underperform in comparison with national averages, remain. The average test scores of African American children are consistently lower than that of white children.

Racism and discrimination are no longer supported by the legal system or cultural norms. But racism and discrimination remain in pockets of US society, sometimes simmering just below the surface of everyday life.

Still, most African Americans have benefited from the civil rights movement. They can travel America's roads and railways without fear of harassment, threats, or violence. They can attend the schools they desire and get the education they need to succeed. They can vote as they please or run for office to implement the changes they seek.

The civil rights movement has forever changed the nature of life for all races in America. The conversation about rights has moved beyond African Americans to focus on ethnicity, gender, and sexual orientation. African Americans and other minorities are woven into the fabric of American life. They sit beside one another on buses and trains. They work beside one another in offices and factories. They live beside one another in city apartments and suburban homes. They come together in elementary schools, high schools, and universities to learn about the nation's shared past, its successes and failures, and where it may be headed in the future.

Source Notes

Introduction: The Defining Characteristics of the Civil Rights Movement

1. Martin Luther King Jr., "I Have a Dream," American Rhetoric: Top 100 Speeches. www.americanrhetoric.com.
2. King, "I Have a Dream."

Chapter One: What Conditions Led to the Civil Rights Movement?

3. Quoted in, "The Untold Story of Emmett Louis Till," documentary directed by Keith Beauchamp, 2005.
4. Tsahai Tafari, "The Rise and Fall of Jim Crow," Educational Broadcasting Corporation, 2002. www.pbs.org.
5. Benjamin W. Arnett, "The Black Laws," speech, Ohio House of Representatives, March 10, 1886. http://memory.loc.gov.
6. Henry Billings Brown, majority opinion, *Plessy v. Ferguson* (163 U.S. 537). http://caselaw.lp.findlaw.com.
7. Brown, majority opinion, *Plessy v. Ferguson*.
8. Quoted in LawBuzz, "Separate but Equal," *Plessy v. Ferguson*, 1896. www.lawbuzz.com.
9. Quoted in LawBuzz, "Separate but Equal."
10. C. Vann Woodward, *The Strange Career of Jim Crow*, 3rd ed. New York: Oxford University Press, 1974, p. 97.
11. Woodward, *The Strange Career of Jim Crow*, p. 100.
12. Vincent Harding, prologue to *The Eyes on the Prize Civil Rights Reader: Documents, Speeches, and Firsthand Accounts from the Black Freedom Struggle, 1954–1990*, Clayborne Carson et al., eds. New York: Penguin, 1991, pp. 25–26.
13. Diane McWhorter, *A Dream of Freedom: The Civil Rights Movement from 1954 to 1968*. New York: Scholastic, 2004, pp. 13–14.

14. Quoted in Henry Hampton and Steve Fayer, *Voices of Freedom: An Oral History of the Civil Rights Movement from the 1950s through the 1980s.* New York: Bantam, 1990, p. 18.

15. Quoted in J. Morgan Kousser, "The Poll Tax," California Institute of Technology. www.hss.caltech.edu.

16. Quoted in Milton Meltzer, *There Comes a Time: The Struggle for Civil Rights.* New York: Random House, 2001, p. 48.

Chapter Two: The Seeds of Resistance

17. Brown Foundation, *Black/White & Brown: Brown versus the Board of Education of Topeka*, transcript, p. 8. http://brownvboard.org /sites/default/files/blackwhitebrown-60min.pdf.

18. Quoted in US Department of State, InfoUSA, "Basic Readings in U.S. Democracy: *Brown v. Board of Education* (1954)." http://us info.state.gov.

19. Quoted in Oyez Project at IIT Chicago–Kent College of Law, *Brown v. Board of Education (II).* www.oyez.org.

20. Quoted in Bill Begelow, "Student Handout: Elizabeth Ann Eckford," Eyes on the Prize, 2003. www.civilrightsteaching.org.

21. Quoted in Herb Boyd, ed., *Autobiography of a People: Three Centuries of African American History Told by Those Who Lived It.* New York: Doubleday, 2000, pp. 369–70.

22. Quoted in Debbie Elliott, "The First Civil Rights Bus Boycott," NPR, June 19, 2003. www.npr.org.

23. Quoted in Bettye Collier-Thomas and V.P. Franklin, eds., *Sisters in the Struggle: African American Women in the Civil Rights–Black Power Movement.* New York: New York University Press, 2001, pp. 67–68.

24. Quoted in Kai Friese, *Rosa Parks: The Movement Organizes.* Englewood Cliffs, NJ: Silver Burdett, 1990, p. 67.

25. Quoted in Hampton and Fayer, *Voices of Freedom*, pp. 25–26.

26. Quoted in Meltzer, *There Comes a Time*, pp. 95–96.

27. Quoted in Hampton and Fayer, *Voices of Freedom*, p. 32.

28. Quoted in Jannell McGrew, "Rev. Robert Graetz," They Changed the World, 1955–1956: The Story of the Montgomery Bus Boycott. www.montgomeryboycott.com.

Chapter Three: The Movement Organizes

29. Quoted in US Marshals Service, "History: U.S. Marshals and the Integration of the University of Mississippi." www.usmarshals.gov.

30. Quoted in Richard D. Mahoney, *Sons & Brothers: The Days of Jack and Bobby Kennedy*. New York: Arcade, 1999, p. 182.

31. Quoted in Mahoney, *Sons & Brothers*, p. 182.

32. Quoted in Mahoney, *Sons & Brothers*, p. 186.

33. Quoted in Shelia Hardwell Byrd, "Meredith Ready to Move On," *Online Athens: Athens Banner-Herald*, September 21, 2002. http://onlineathens.com.

34. George C. Wallace, "The 1963 Inaugural Address of Governor George C. Wallace," Alabama Department of Archives & History, January 14, 1963. www.archives.alabama.gov.

35. Quoted in Claude Sitton, "Alabama Admits Negro Students; Wallace Bows to Federal Force; Kennedy Sees 'Moral Crisis' in U.S." *New York Times on the Web*, June 12, 1963. http://movies.nytimes.com.

36. Quoted in Sitton, "Alabama Admits Negro Students."

37. Quoted in *BlackPressUSA*, "Heisman Award Does Not Hide Alabama's Past," Op-Ed. www.blackpressusa.com.

38. Woodward, *The Strange Career of Jim Crow*, p. 100.

39. Wyatt Tee Walker, interview by Blackside, Inc. in Eyes on the Prize: America's Civil Rights Years (1954–1965), Washington University Libraries, "Film and Media Archive," Henry Hampton Collection, October 11, 1985. http://digital.wustl.edu.

40. Quoted in Andrew M. Manis, *A Fire You Can't Put Out: The Civil Rights Life of Birmingham's Reverend Fred Shuttlesworth*. Tuscaloosa: University of Alabama Press, 1999, p. 387.

41. Quoted in PBS, "Patience Is a Dirty and Nasty Word," *Primary Sources*, August 28, 1963. www.pbs.org.

42. King, "I Have a Dream."

Chapter Four: The Struggle Intensifies

43. McWhorter, *A Dream of Freedom*, p. 100.

44. Quoted in Douglas O. Linder, "Bending Toward Justice: John Doar and the Mississippi Burning Trial," *Mississippi Law Journal,* Winter 2002. http://law2.umkc.edu.

45. Quoted in American RadioWorks, "State of Siege: The Citizens' Council," American Public Media. http://americanradioworks .publicradio.org.

46. Quoted in American RadioWorks, "State of Siege: The Citizens' Council."

47. Quoted in Kate Ellis and Stephen Smith, "State of Siege: Mississippi Whites and the Civil Rights Movement," American Radio-Works, American Public Media, 2012. http://americanradioworks .publicradio.org.

48. Quoted in American RadioWorks, "State of Siege: The Citizens' Council."

49. Quoted in Linder, "Bending Toward Justice."

50. Quoted in Linder, "Bending Toward Justice."

51. Andrew Goodman Foundation, "History," www.andrewgoodman .org.

52. John Lewis, *Walking with the Wind: A Memoir of the Movement.* New York: Simon & Schuster, 1998, p. 291.

53. Lewis, *Walking with the Wind,* p. 291.

54. Malcolm X, "By Any Means Necessary," YouTube video, 7:39, NewsOne, Top 5 Malcom X Speeches, from a speech at Audubon Ballroom, Harlem, New York, February 21, 1965. http://newsone .com/184281/top-5-malcom-x-speeches.

55. Quoted in Voxygen.net, "Malcolm X Ballot or the Bullet Speech," April 3, 1964. http://voxygen.net.

56. Quoted in *Encyclopedia Britannica's Guide to Black History,* "Advice to the Youth of Mississippi," 1964. www.britannica.com.

57. Stokely Carmichael, "Black Power Address at UC Berkeley, October 1966," American Rhetoric: Top 100 Speeches. www.american rhetoric.com.

58. Quoted in Gordon Parks, "Whip of Black Power," *Life,* May 19, 1967, p. 82.

59. Quoted in Jeffrey G. Ogbar, *Black Power: Radical Politics and African American Identity*. Baltimore: Johns Hopkins University Press, 2004, p. 64.

60. Bayard Ruslin, "The Watts," *Commentary,* March 1966. http://www.commentarymagazine.com.

61. Martin Luther King Jr., "A Christmas Sermon on Peace," in *A Testament of Hope: The Essential Writings and Speeches of Martin Luther King Jr.*, James M. Washington, ed. New York: HarperOne, 1990, p. 57.

62. Quoted in SocialistAlternative.Org, "The Black Panther Party," www.socialstalternative.org.

63. Martin Luther King Jr., "I've Been to the Mountaintop," American Rhetoric: Top 100 Speeches, April 3, 1968. www.americanrhetoric.com.

Chapter Five: What Is the Legacy of the Civil Rights Movement?

64. John F. Kennedy, "Executive Order 10925: Establishing the President's Committee on Equal Employment Opportunity," March 6, 1961. www.eeoc.gov.

65. Lyndon B. Johnson, "Equal Opportunity Is Not Enough," Howard University commencement address, in *Eyes on the Prize: America's Civil Rights Movement, 1954–1985*, PBS. www.pbs.org.

66. Franklin D. Roosevelt, Executive Order 8802: "Prohibition of Discrimination in the Defense Industry," June 25, 1941. www.eeoc.gov.

67. Quoted in National Park Service, "The Prize," *We Shall Overcome: Historic Places of the Civil Rights Movement.* www.nps.gov.

68. Virginia Historical Society, "The Legacy of the Civil Rights Movement," *The Civil Rights Movement in Virginia.* www.vahistorical.org.

Important People in the Civil Rights Movement

Ralph Abernathy: A close associate of Martin Luther King Jr., Abernathy was a cofounder of the Southern Christian Leadership Conference. He led the SCLC Poor People's Campaign and the 1968 March on Washington that was held following King's assassination.

Stokely Carmichael: Following his participation in the 1961 Freedom Rides, Carmichael became a leader of the Student Nonviolent Coordinating Committee. Carmichael was a staunch advocate of black power, which he defined as African Americans coming together to form a political force.

Martin Luther King Jr.: King rose to prominence as the leader of the Montgomery, Alabama, bus boycott and remained one of the most influential people of the civil rights movement until his 1968 assassination. King was a cofounder of the Southern Christian Leadership Conference and became known for his commitment to nonviolent resistance and for his outstanding speaking skills.

Malcolm X: Born Malcolm Little, Malcolm took X as his last name when he joined the Nation of Islam and became a black nationalist. In contrast to the nonviolent tactics espoused by most leaders of the civil rights movement, Malcolm X urged African Americans to take their rights by any means necessary.

Thurgood Marshall: Marshall was one of the primary lawyers who successfully argued *Brown v. Board of Education*, in which the Supreme Court overturned its defense of separate but equal facilities in *Plessy* *v. Ferguson* and declared segregation in schools unconstitutional. Marshall went on to become the first African American Supreme Court justice in American history.

James Meredith: In 1962 Meredith became the first black student to successfully enroll at the University of Mississippi. Riots broke out in response, causing President Kennedy to send five thousand federal troops to restore the peace.

Rosa Parks: Parks, an NAACP member, made history in 1955 when she refused to give up her seat on a segregated bus in Montgomery, Alabama, for a white passenger. After her arrest the black community launched a bus boycott that lasted more than a year and ended with the desegregation of Montgomery's buses on December 21, 1956.

Emmett Till: Fourteen-year-old Emmett Till became an important symbol for the civil rights movement when he was violently murdered by white men after allegedly whistling at a white woman. Despite overwhelming evidence of their guilt, the two white men accused of his murder were acquitted by an all-white jury.

For Further Research

Books

Daniel W. Aldridge, *Becoming American: The African American Quest for Civil Rights, 1861–1976*. Wheeling, IL: Harlan Davidson, 2011.

Julie Buckner Armstrong and Amy Schmidt, *The Civil Rights Reader: American Literature from Jim Crow to Reconciliation*. Atlanta: University of Georgia Press, 2009.

Maurice Berger, *For All the World to See: Visual Culture and the Struggle for Civil Rights*. New Haven, CT: Yale University Press, 2010.

David C. Carter, *The Music Has Gone Out of the Movement: Civil Rights and the Johnson Administration, 1965–1968*. Chapel Hill: University of North Carolina Press, 2009.

Dorothy Cotton, *If Your Back's Not Bent: How the Civil Rights Movement Gained Victory*. New York: Atria, 2012.

Catherine Ellis and Stephen Drury Smith, *Say It Loud: Great Speeches on Civil Rights and African American Identity*. New York: New Press, 2010.

Linda Barrett Osborne, *Miles to Go for Freedom: Segregation and Civil Rights in the Jim Crow Years*. New York: Abrams, 2012.

William T. Martin Riches, *The Civil Rights Movement: Struggle and Resistance*. 3rd ed. New York: Palgrave Macmillan, 2010.

Patricia Sullivan, *Lift Every Voice: The NAACP and the Making of the Civil Rights Movement*. New York: New Press, 2010.

Websites

Amistad Digital Resource: Civil Rights Era (www.amistadresource
.org/civil_rights_era). Created by Columbia University for use by teachers, this website provides detailed background information about the
civil rights movement and the key people and organizations involved,
as well as primary source documents, images, videos, and audio.

Civil Rights in America: Connections to a Movement (http://topics
.gannett.com/civil+rights/?template=clarionledger). With a focus on
the stories of people living before, during, and after the civil rights
movement, this website includes digitized newspaper pages, archived
records, documents, and videos on the civil rights movement along
with rich context provided from newspapers and television stations
that were there at the movement's height.

Civil Rights Movement (www.history.com/topics/civil-rights-move
ment). The History Channel's website provides written information
and videos about the people and events of the civil rights movement.

Civil Rights Movement Veterans (www.crmvet.org). This site tells of
the civil rights movement from the perspective of those who participated in the southern freedom movement and includes information
for students, timelines, documents and letters, discussion questions, a
bibliography, web links, and a variety of other information.

Library of Congress Civil Rights Resource Guide (www.loc.gov/rr
/program/bib/civilrights/home.html). The Library of Congress's digital collections contain a wide variety of material related to civil rights,
including photographs, documents, and sound recordings, as well as a
bibliography and links to external websites for further study.

Martin Luther King Jr. Research and Education Institute (http://mlk
-kpp01.stanford.edu/index.php/resources/index.php). Created and
maintained by Stanford University, this site provides a wealth of information about Martin Luther King Jr. and the people and events of the

civil rights movement in a wide variety of formats. Included are audio-visual materials, sermons and speeches, photo galleries, lesson plans, and student resources and study guides.

The Rise and Fall of Jim Crow (www.pbs.org/wnet/jimcrow/struggle .html). This PBS site focuses on life in the South before the civil rights movement and the events that contributed to growing resistance to seg-regation.

State of Siege: Mississippi Whites and the Civil Rights Movement (http://americanradioworks.publicradio.org/features/mississippi). This site, hosted by American RadioWorks, describes the fierce tactics by which citizen groups and state agencies in Mississippi fought to maintain racial segregation.

We Shall Overcome: Historic Places of the Civil Rights Movement (www.nps.gov/nr/travel/civilrights). This National Parks Service site provides background information about the civil rights movement and the events leading up to it, as well as a virtual tour of the many places related to the movement's history.

Index

Picture Credits

Cover: AP Images

AP Images: 9, 37, 44, 59, 79

© Bettmann/Corbis: 17, 22, 27, 33, 53, 65

© Saul Loeb/Pool/Corbis: 71

Thinkstock: 6, 7

Steve Zmina: 11, 46

About the Author

Lydia Bjornlund is a freelance writer and editor living in Northern Virginia. She has written more than two dozen nonfiction books for children and teens, mostly on American history and health-related topics. She also writes books and training materials for adults on issues related to land conservation, emergency management, and public policy. Bjornlund holds a master's degree in education from Harvard University and a BA in American Studies from Williams College. She lives with her husband, Gerry Hoetmer, and their children, Jake and Sophia.